Pit to Power Station

A Personal Recollection of Coal Trains in the 1990s

CHRIS BOOTH

Fonthill Media Language Policy

Fonthill Media publishes in the international English language market. One language edition is published worldwide. As there are minor differences in spelling and presentation, especially with regard to American English and British English, a policy is necessary to define which form of English to use. The Fonthill Policy is to use the form of English native to the author. Chris Booth was born and educated in Worksop, Nottinghamshire; therefore, British English has been adopted in this publication.

Fonthill Media Limited
Fonthill Media LLC
www.fonthill.media
books@fonthill.media

First published in the United Kingdom and the United States of America 2022

British Library Cataloguing in Publication Data:
A catalogue record for this book is available from the British Library

Copyright © Chris Booth 2022

ISBN 978-1-78155-866-9

The right of Chris Booth to be identified as the author of this work has been asserted by him in accordance with the Copyright, Designs and Patents Act 1988.

All rights reserved. No part of this publication may be reproduced, stored in a retrieval system or transmitted in any form or by any means, electronic, mechanical, photocopying, recording or otherwise, without prior permission in writing from Fonthill Media Limited

Typeset in 10pt on 13pt Sabon
Printed and bound in England

Acknowledgements

Although the majority of photographs are my own, I must thank the following for their help with paperwork relating to coal traffic, from which I have gleaned a lot of material. In no particular order, they are: Dafydd Whyles, Neil Baker, James Skoyles, Derek Talbot, and Barry Taylor.

Thanks to Nick Allsop for forwarding a copy of a Willington power station diagram sent to him by Ian Farnfield, an ex-Coalville driver. I must also thank Greg Sherlock for proofreading and editing the text, and finally thanks to Robin Stewart-Smith for photos of the construction of Worksop Depot.

Contents

Acknowledgements — 3
Introduction — 7

1. Worksop in the 1980s and 1990s: The Decades of Change — 13
2. Declining UK Coal Production — 42
3. Nottinghamshire Area Collieries — 56
4. Derbyshire Area Collieries — 109
5. Yorkshire Area Collieries — 133
6. Leicestershire and Staffordshire Area Collieries — 183
7. Power Stations — 192
8. Three Days at Worksop — 241

Bibliography — 256

Introduction

I have had an interest in railways since the age of seven, when I was first taken to Retford station on the crossbar of my cousin Brian's bike to watch the steam and diesel-hauled expresses thundering through. As I got older, my friend Alan Hazell and I would often visit Worksop station and sit on one of the parcels trolleys to watch proceedings, getting told off by the porters for moving their trolley into different positions. My interest continued through the years, and Alan and I would travel all over the country trainspotting.

My dad was a miner, and we lived very close to Manton Colliery, so I would watch the miners walking to and from work and, with my dad, would very often visit the canteen and wages office. While he went in to get his wages, I would wander around and watch the coal wagons being shunted under the screens. Could you imagine the furore if a ten-year-old was wandering around a working mine today?

As school leaving age arrived, I had to make a decision on future employment. My initial thoughts were to follow in my dad's footsteps and work down the pit, but he had other ideas and did not want me to due to the inherent dangers of mining. Instead, I went to Worksop station and enquired about a job on the railways as, by then, they were my passion. Sadly, at that time, there were no vacancies, and so I took a job as an apprentice butcher with the Co-op, which saw me work in the slaughterhouse, on mobile vans, and in shops.

The trade did not really suit me, and within three years, I had changed jobs. The railways still had no vacancies, so I ended up at Carlton Cycles, a Worksop-based manufacturer that was part of the Raleigh empire. Two years later, I heard rumours of impending redundancies in the factory, so to pre-empt things, I once again visited the BR office, with success this time, and soon after, I began work with British Rail in June 1975 as a pupil at the signalling school in Retford.

My first position was as a signalman at Dinnington Colliery Junction on the freight-only former South Yorkshire Joint Railway line between Brancliffe East Junction and Maltby.

This line was predominantly a coal-carrying line from the many collieries in the area, and it was then I began to take more of an interest in coal trains.

Moving to Worksop Sidings signal box in 1977, I then worked more closely with coal trains as this controlled Worksop Yards, with its many shunting moves for coal trains in and out of the yard.

I moved to Worksop West Junction in 1981, staying there until it closed in 1997, after which I moved to my final position at Worksop power signal box, where I continued to deal with coal along with the passenger traffic.

I have authored many articles in the railway press since 1994, when I had my first article published. Since that time, I have authored three books about *The Lancashire, Derbyshire, and East Coast Railway* (Fonthill Media) and co-authored another entitled *Tinsley and the Modernisation of Sheffield's Railways* (Platform 5 Publishing).

Initially, my interests in photography were limited to the odd train photographed at the boxes I worked or out and about, but these were mainly locomotive portraits. As the closure of collieries accelerated in the 1990s, I began seeking out places within easy travelling distance to photograph the trains serving them, along with the power stations they supplied coal to. Since then, I have amassed a large number of photos of coal traffic, and the idea of this book is to show some of them.

I have picked the 1990s primarily because it was a time of change, and the collieries and several of the power stations of that era have now gone—so too have the locomotives utilised at the time, all but vanishing from main line operations. In the main, these were Classes 56, 58, and 60, but with some Class 20s still featuring in small numbers.

This was originally to be a showcase for my photos taken at the collieries as they were closing, but it developed into a potted history of the decimation of the coal industry and how Worksop Depot changed in the 1990s. I hope you enjoy reminiscing about the coal trains in the 1990s as much as I enjoyed putting the book together.

Chris Booth
Worksop, 2021

One of my earliest coal train photos sees No. 56011 passing the original Midland Railway, Woodend Junction down home signals with an empty set of wagons for Creswell Colliery on a dull day in 1978.

Introduction

Dawn breaks over Worksop as viewed from Worksop Sidings box on a cold November morning in 1979. A Class 31 waits further duties while Ken Hopkinson, the downside shunter, has just emerged from his cabin. Meanwhile in the background, a Class 08 shunts the MGR depot.

As dawn breaks on 12 November 1990, blue-liveried 56004 with 6F37 Cottam to Worksop is stood at Worksop West No. 1 signal, waiting a clear reception siding. This image was published on the front cover of the *East Midlands Freight* magazine.

Passing Worksop West (my place of work at the time), 20075 and 20057 make hard work of the 1-in-300 gradient while working 7F39 Thurcroft to Cottam on 17 January 1992.

Photographing the Trains

Although I do have a few earlier coal train photos, my interest in photographing these at collieries really took off from 1993 after many had closed and had been demolished, with just the coal stocks to remove. I subsequently missed the collieries close to my area that closed—namely Shireoaks (which closed in 1990); Creswell, Dinnington, Gedling, and Thurcroft (in 1991); and Shirebrook, Sherwood, and Silverhill (in 1992). As such, these are the collieries or remains of collieries I visited and photographed between 1993 and 1999, the furthest away being Silverdale in Staffordshire.

Closed in 1993: Bentley, Bolsover, Frickley, Rufford and Sharlston.
Closed in 1994: Goldthorpe, Kiveton Park, Markham (Derbyshire), Manton, and Ollerton.
Closed in 1995: Bilsthorpe.
Closed in 1996: Markham Main (Yorkshire).
Closed in 1997: None.
Closed in 1998: Silverdale.
Closed in 1999: Calverton.

Other collieries photographed that closed after 2000 were Clipstone, Hatfield, Thoresby, and Welbeck, so there will be views of these taken during the 1990s. The collieries featured will be in the order of county and alphabetical order, starting with the Nottinghamshire area.

There was heavy snow, gales, and freezing temperatures during the winter of 1990–91. December saw a lot of snow countrywide that caused much disruption to travel. January and February saw more freezing temperatures and snow that then began to thaw, subsequently re-freezing at night. By 20 February, warmer air was arriving but there was still a lot of laying snow as witnessed here as 58049 *Littleton Colliery* is entering No. 1 up reception at Shireoaks East Junction on 25 January 1991.

The railway usually continued through the worst weather. Here, 58023 leaves Worksop down reception No. 2 with 6F61 empty set for Manton during a blizzard on 23 February 1994.

1

Worksop in the 1980s and 1990s: The Decades of Change

As a British Rail employee based in Worksop, I worked through the turbulent 1980s with the miners' strike (and its consequences), the formation of Trainload Coal and East Midlands Freight, and, as the 1990s arrived, the major differences that came to the nationalised railways and the coal industry. What follows is just an overview of the situation during the late 1980s and into the 1990s as I saw it in the Worksop area.

The 1990s was a decade of change as railways were gearing up for privatisation and eventual sale, which saw the track and signalling infrastructure side go to Railtrack, while the movement of coal in the Worksop area went first to shadow privatisation company Mainline Freight, then to the American-owned giant English, Welsh & Scottish Railways.

Railfreight Coal

The story begins in 1982 with the formation of Railfreight Coal, when British Rail went through a re-organisation and implemented its 'sectorisation' program of splitting up the company itself into a number of separate business entities. This resulted in the creation of Intercity, Network SouthEast, Provincial (later renamed Regional Railways), Parcels, and Railfreight.

Railfreight was later sub-divided and named according to the type of goods they transported—*i.e.* Railfreight Coal, Construction, Metals, Petroleum, and Distribution. Each of these sub-sectors had their own management with Railfreight Coal having over 200 locomotives and over 11,000 specialised wagons all dedicated to the bulk movement of coal. The sectors, although given their 'individuality', were still under the direct control of Railfreight (BR) and the British Rail Board.

A new livery was unveiled on Class 58 locomotive 58001 when it was introduced to service in 1983, becoming known as 'Red Stripe Railfreight', and the debut of the livery at Worksop was when 58004 arrived light engine from Doncaster for evaluation in September 1983.

Towards the end of the 1980s, thoughts turned to a new look image for the businesses. The task was given to the design consultation company 'Roundel Design Group', who came up with the 'triple grey' livery together with a series of logos to denote the major commodity carried by each sector. The six new logos were designed in connection with the DM&EE and Freight Division headquarters in Derby and consisted of:

Railfreight General—red and yellow lines
Railfreight Distribution—red and yellow diamonds
Coal—black diamonds representing coal
Petroleum—blue and yellow wavy lines representing fluid
Construction—blue and yellow squares representing building blocks
Metals—blue and yellow chevrons representing corrugated iron

The Trainload sector symbols as designed by the Roundel Design Group.

No. 58019 is framed by bridge No. 68 Southfield Lane at Whitwell, as it passes Whitwell station signal box and heads for Creswell with 6G64 Worksop to Creswell Colliery on 9 November 1987. The signalman on duty was Gordon Bennett and his Talbot Horizon car waits adjacent to the goods shed, which at that time was in use by a paper recycling company.

No. 58039 *Rugeley Power Station* is seen just after leaving Whitwell tunnel while working 7F57 from Shirebrook to Cottam power station on a murky 9 November 1987.

BR blue livery 56015 is passing Worksop station with 7G36 for West Burton power station on a dull 13 May 1988, the station canopies were in dire need of some remedial attention at this time.

Supporting Trainload Coal sector branding 56007 passes the signals at Worksop West with 6G42 Immingham to Worksop on 28 July 1993.

East Midlands Freight

In April 1987, the Derby, Leicester, and Nottingham areas were reorganised into East Midlands Passenger (based at Derby) and East Midlands Freight (based at Toton), and by the end of the year, Railfreight Coal was moving 500,000 tons of coal per week in the Nottinghamshire East Midlands Freight area alone. Late 1988–early 1989 saw a rebranding exercise take place where the Railfreight business name officially became known as Trainload Freight. The Railfreight Coal, Construction, Metals, and Petroleum sub-sectors became known as Trainload Coal, Construction, Metals, and Petroleum respectively. The only Railfreight sector that did not become a Trainload business was Railfreight Distribution, which continued as a subsidiary of the BR Board.

The national business manager for Trainload Coal was Kim Jordan, overseeing business managers based in York and Nottingham, the latter area having three managers overseeing operations in South Wales, the North-West, and the East Midlands. This book will primarily be concerned with parts of the latter, although other areas such as Yorkshire and Derbyshire will also be touched upon.

The East Midlands area was managed by Tim Gilbert, the area extending from the Coalville line in Leicestershire, through Toton, to Worksop and over the South Yorkshire line almost to Doncaster. At that time, the area contained nine power stations, twenty-four deep mines, and several opencast disposal points.

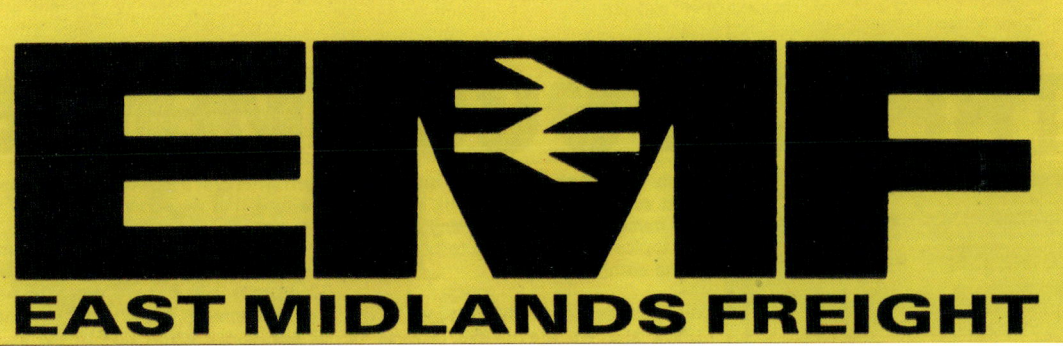

East Midlands Freight masthead.

Yorkshire Freight area tie showing the Yorkshire Freight logo.

Yorkshire Freight

The northern extremity of East Midlands Freight was on the South Yorkshire Joint Line between Brancliffe East Junction and Doncaster, after which it became the Yorkshire freight area. The Yorkshire freight area manager was former Worksop-based Eric Straw, who was responsible for an area that included Tinsley, Doncaster, Healey Mills, and Knottingley, with the latter crews being primarily responsible for working trains to the Aire Valley power stations at Ferrybridge, Eggborough, and Drax.

Worksop Depot

Worksop train crew depot was opened in June 1965, when Retford Thrumpton steam depot closed and the men were transferred. One of the first drivers to see the new depot building was George Pickford, who also had the pleasure of claiming the first locker.

By the early 1980s, there was a daily requirement for around thirty engines, which included at least three pairs of Class 20s, at least four Class 31s, around five Class 37s, three Class 08 pilot locos (Up side, Down side, and wagon repair depot), and several Class 56s prior to 1984, after which the Class 58s began to dominate the scene.

Depots had designated pits to work to, there being a demarcation line that was not usually crossed. It was said that Toton crews had joked about there being a 'Berlin Wall' or an 'Iron Curtain' that existed between the London Midland and Eastern Regions. This metaphorical 'boundary' was probably more self-evident at Shirebrook; although the station had closed, so-called 'inter-regional' coal traffic stopped there as it was the furthest south Worksop drivers would work, and in the other direction was the furthest north Toton drivers would work. In the late 1980s, Worksop men worked

Manton, Shireoaks, Kiveton, Dinnington, Thurcroft, and Harworth collieries, taking coal to Cottam and West Burton power stations. They also worked export coal to Immingham via the South Yorkshire Joint line and Doncaster.

The pits served by Shirebrook staff included Welbeck, Warsop, Shirebrook, Sutton, Ollerton, Thoresby, and Bevercotes, together with those along the former Mansfield Railway at Clipstone, Bilsthorpe, Rufford, and Crown Farm. These latter pits were dual-served, and Toton men would work trains out from the former London Midland side via Mansfield South Junction. Shirebrook crews worked to Toton with Northfleet-bound coal traffic from Thoresby and Welbeck; they also worked export coal to Immingham but were routed via Worksop and Brigg—never via the South Yorkshire Joint Line. The drivers also had turns to Whitemoor via Pyewipe Junction (until the former LD&ECR line closed beyond High Marnham power station in 1980), Willington, Derby, Burton-upon-Trent, Avenue Coking Plant, and other diagrams, including via Woodend Junction to Beighton, Rotherwood, and Tinsley.

It was a closed shop until the rules changed with the advent of Trainload Coal, when the depot nearest the receiving power station became responsible for collection from the source and delivery to the user. According to the drivers, 'this saved Shirebrook and then Worksop from invasion by Immingham and Toton men!'

Worksop and Barrow Hill men called Shirebrook depot 'The Happy Valley', hence the staff were known as valley men. Former Shirebrook driver Robert (Bob) Wigley thought that was 'probably because we dashed around and overtime was unheard of, no Rest Day Working, and no weekend work except for Sunday ballast turns.'

No. 58034 *Bassetlaw* and 58020 are seen on Shirebrook depot on 6 May 1995.

No. 58040 *Cottam Power Station* and 58026 inside Shirebrook depot 23 May 1996.

New Depot

In 1990, Trainload Coal planned to construct a new train crew depot at Worksop to pool the drivers of Worksop, Shirebrook, and Barrow Hill. Barrow Hill Roundhouse would close, but Shirebrook TMD would remain in use for the foreseeable future. The reasoning was that Worksop would become the second most important Trainload Coal depot after Toton, with more services to and from Immingham and the remaining collieries. Worksop would assume responsibility for around twenty Type 5 locos for coal traffic along with Classes 31 and 37 for trip workings, with a staff of around 200. As many as forty-six locos could be allocated to Worksop-based traffic in the 1990s.

The new train crew depot was situated in the former Down side coal yard, the area latterly being used by a second-hand railway sleeper proprietor. With steelwork completed by October 1990, opening took place on 11 February 1991. Its curved roof was said to be loosely designed to look like a Southern Region *Queen Mary* brake van. The fact that locos still required fuelling and maintenance at Shirebrook was to prove expensive as in a twelve-hour period, it was not unknown for up to fifty light engine movements to be made between Worksop and Shirebrook.

Bassetlaw District Council refused planning permission for a fuelling point at Worksop, citing instances of pollution in water courses. In due course, this stance was relaxed in 1996, permitting construction of a concrete pad for the standage of road fuel tankers, complete with drainage into a capture pit. Work commenced on Monday, 3 February 1993, with completion on 17 April. Further planning relaxation later saw a bespoke static fuel tank erected, allowing locos to be fuelled either in the Down yard or on Down Reception No. 2 line.

An artist's impression of the new train crew building at Worksop. (*Author's collection*)

The new steelwork for the Worksop depot traincrew facility is seen on 23 October 1990. (*Robin Stewart-Smith*)

Worksop traincrew depot under construction during November 1990. (*Robin Stewart-Smith*)

New fuelling point under construction in the former coal yard area of Worksop downside during 1997.

With the traincrew depot building in the background, the new fuelling point is under construction at Worksop in 1997.

The First Nail in the Coffin?

In addition to the local collieries, Worksop drivers also worked traffic to Drakelow, Willington, Staythorpe, Ratcliffe, Drax, Ferrybridge, Eggborough, Cottam, West Burton, and Didcot power stations. For the Didcot traffic, they worked the train as far as Landore Street Junction in Birmingham, where they were relieved by men from Saltley Depot. Ironbridge power station traffic was also worked as far as Toton.

The opening of Worksop depot was designed to bring new life to the area, but after a lull, colliery closures recommenced. Shireoaks closed in 1990, with Creswell, Dinnington, and Thurcroft following in 1991, the first of many such closures to come that had an impact on Worksop drivers, with a consequent reduction in traffic.

With 50,000 tonnes of stock on the surface, all destined for Avenue coking plant near Chesterfield, Dinnington's final train left the colliery for Avenue as 7Z32 at 9.20 a.m. on 13 February 1992, with 58037 at the helm. Thurcroft Colliery had 30,000 tonnes of stock for Cottam power station and dispatched its final train in thick fog at 2.35 p.m. on 31 January 1992 as 7F47, hauled by 20168 and 20128.

The use of Class 20s on Thurcroft traffic was regular as Worksop had three Trainload Coal-sponsored pairs at the time, the others being 20007 and 20032 with 20169 and 20215. Being fitted with slow speed control, they were used on Cottam trains, where the sound of them clattering up Welham bank between Retford and Clarborough could be heard for miles. As the Class 60s were introduced, the Class 20s were threatened with withdrawal.

On 21 September 1992, Trainload Coal held a private naming ceremony at Worksop in which two Class 60s were named after the main instigators of the merry-go-round

The secondman of 20072 and 20187 hands the staff for the Thurcroft branch to Ray Williams as he is passing Dinnington Colliery box on 15 January 1992. Thurcroft was worked by Class 20s to the end.

Nos 20075 and 20057 approach Worksop West, returning from Cottam with an empty MGR set on 16 January 1992, just two months before they would be transferred away from Worksop.

A line up of Class 20s at Worksop on 2 February 1992. Nos 20128, 20168, 20032, and 20007 wait further duties a few weeks before all the Class 20s left Worksop.

system, namely 60092 *Reginald Munns* and 60093 *Jack Stirk*. Mr Munns was BR's national coal manager from 1969 to 1982, and it was due to his work with the National Coal Board (NCB) and Central Electricity Generating Board (CEGB) that the initial experiments were made with merry-go-round (MGR) operation at West Burton power station, which led to the major development of the MGR operation and subsequent contracts to move coal by rail. Mr Stirk was the coal board manager who co-ordinated the implementation of the MGR system and negotiated the long-term contracts with the CEGB, which ensured the overall commercial success.

The closure of Avenue coking plant at Clay Cross also reduced Worksop's workload. The final train worked into the plant on 14 September 1992, with the closure announcement being made by British Coal on 13 October 1992.

Further staff reductions were made in 1992. At that time, train preparers (TPs) on three shift workings were based at those collieries that warranted them due to traffic demands, but in 1992 they were removed from their colliery bases and given yellow BR vans to travel between locations as travelling train preparers (TTPs).

By March 1993, the Trainload Coal sector locomotive fleet consisted of one Class 47, six Class 20s, nine Class 31s, forty-one Class 37s, eighty-one Class 56s, fifty Class 58s, and thirty-five Class 60s. However, Worksop depot lost its Class 20 compliment from 13 March 1992. There were fourteen Class 60s allotted to Worksop traffic with a requirement of twelve per day. These were used on coal from Welbeck to Didcot, Hunslet (Leeds, where they were required due to the gradients on the Hunslet branch) imported coal from Warrington, and occasional local traffic such as to Oxcroft Opencast disposal point.

Above: No. 60092 *Reginald Munns* and 60093 *Jack Stirk* waiting the following day's naming at Worksop down side on 20 September 1992.

Below left: As 58010 approaches Holbrook crossing with 7C47 on the 8.25 a.m. Denby for Drakelow, Wayne Woods, the travelling train preparer, waits for it to cross on 15 March 1999.

Below right: The travelling train preparers van sits alongside 58033 sporting EW&S red livery while it is loading 7F86 on the 10.41 a.m. Manton to Cottam on 27 September 1996. This was the first train out of Manton Colliery since September 1995. The van is registered H299 YHM, the 'H' meaning it was registered between August 1990 and July 1991.

It is important to note at this point that many of the locomotive classes listed above were fitted with slow speed control. This feature was one part of the jigsaw that made the MGR operation the success that it was. Trains were signalled normally into the power station boundary until the approach to the unloading bunker. The power station control room would then give the driver instructions via special lineside signals as to whether to stop or proceed, etc. At this point, the driver would engage the slow speed control and, when proceeding normally through the unloading bunker, the train would crawl forward at 0.5 mph.

The HAA wagons and their derivatives (mentioned in greater detail further in this chapter) would have their bottom discharge doors unlocked, opened for discharge, closed and locked again by fixed lineside equipment that engaged with wagon-mounted levers. Most power stations mentioned in this book were equipped for MGR operation.

Worksop Open Day Committee Formed

The first open day was held at Worksop on 6 June 1987 when, in conjunction with Shirebrook depot, exhibits were displayed at both locations with a series of shuttle trains running between the two. This was the impetus for the formation of the Worksop open day committee in 1991 with founding members Barry Taylor and Dave Hindson, together with Sandra Haldon, Dave Jones, Tommy Taylor, and Jack Wilson.

On 1 September 1991, a second Worksop depot open day was held, and a series of highly successful special trains were run on the day from Chesterfield and Doncaster. This was the incentive needed for the Worksop charity train committee to be formed and run a series of trains over the years with the aim of raising funds for charity. Worksop drivers and route conductors from various depots worked the trains throughout. With destinations including Blair Atholl, Ayr, Edinburgh, Aberystwyth, Margate, Weymouth, and Paignton, £269,811 was raised mostly for local Bassetlaw area charities.

The furthest north that the Worksop charity train committee organised a train to was Blair Atholl on the Highland Mainline on 29 June 2002. Here, 58025 and 58045 are seen with the *Worksop Highlander* after running around the train at Blair Atholl as tour participants stretch their legs.

Privatisation Looms

The decline of the coal industry in the early 1990s saw the Trainload Coal sector in a state of flux, as this period was one of transition with the privatisation of the railways, and British Rail being broken up into over 100 separate companies. It was also a time of the privatisation of the electricity industry.

With the impending privatisation of the railways, a letter dated 27 May 1993 was sent out to all employees of East Midlands Freight from the area manager, Tim Edwards:

Dear Colleague
FREIGHT PRIVATISATION ANNOUNCEMENT
Since the issue of East Midlands Freight went to print last week, the Government has made its long-awaited announcement on freight privatisation. The proposals were announced in the House of Commons on Thursday 20 May 1993 by Secretary of State for Transport, John MacGregor. Briefly, the key points affecting us are as follows:—

Trainload Freight and Railfreight Distributions Contract Services are to be formed into three new competing companies based on a South East/North East/West geographic division of existing services.

The necessary restructuring is to start immediately, with a target completion date of APRIL 1994.

A period of operational running in the public sector (i.e. as part of British Rail) will then follow before any decision on the method of privatisation is made and implemented.

Departmental locos and wagons (i.e. for ballast etc.) will transfer to the new companies.

RfD's Freightliner and European services will continue with BR (i.e. not form part of the three new companies), for the foreseeable future.

New freight operators will be free to compete with BR from April 1994 subject to them meeting certain criteria regarding safety etc.

These points are only the bare-bones of the ministerial announcement, which covered several other areas including Rail Express Systems and Red Star.

The statement did not deal with matters in detail. For example, the boundaries of the new companies have not been specified, with only a broad indication of which areas will be covered by which companies. However, it appears clear that for us, the intention is that those parts of East Midlands Freight which will not be transferred into the new 'Railtrack' organisations, (signal boxes and line of route control), are likely to become part of the new 'Railfreight South East' operating company. I say 'likely', because no decisions have been taken on this or other matters.

Obviously, the magnitude of the proposals will take a while to settle in. The decisions have been made, by the Government, after consultation with key groups, including our customers. Whatever our personal views about privatisation, we must accept that these changes WILL happen. The proposals are workable and our job is now to implement them. There is a phenomenal workload to be undertaken, however, if the new companies are to be 'up and running' in the timescales indicated. Trainload Freight managers have been charged with setting-up the necessary structures and managing the changes, with the requirement of meeting the specified deadline of 4th April 1994.

My first objective now, is to keep my promise, and commence a briefing cascade with the aim of reaching every member of staff across the East Midlands Freight area. Managers have already been briefed and I have already called Area Council staff representatives to an early meeting to discuss the proposals and implications openly and honestly. The Safety Briefings held at Worksop, Toton and Leicester will be used to convey the details of the announcement to you all.

I know that every member of staff will have questions to ask, both about the future for the industry and the implications for each one of us. We will try to answer your concerns with honesty, although it must be understood that much has yet to be decided upon.

My initial message is 'DON'T PANIC!' At least we now know the intentions of the Government and can plan accordingly. There will clearly be major change in the coming months, but the necessary restructuring is not intended to be an opportunity for massive job cuts or the like.

Obviously I am disappointed that all the plans that we had in place to further develop East Midlands Freight as the premier freight area, will not now come to pass. Just as we were beginning to settle down after our last big reorganisation, only twelve months ago, it is sad that we must now plan to uproot everything once again. However, there is no point in 'crying in our beer'. Our best tactic must be now to accept that the changes will happen and work together, management and staff, to preserve all the best features of our area, and our industry, as the transfer to the new undertakings starts to take place.

ABOVE ALL ELSE, WE MUST REMEMBER OUR OVERRIDING COMMITMENT TO RUNNING A SAFE AND PROFESSIONAL RAILWAY DURING THE MONTHS OF CHANGE THAT LIE AHEAD. NOTHING WOULD DO MORE DAMAGE TO OUR INDUSTRY THAN IF WE WERE TO TAKE OUR 'EYE OFF THE BALL' AND LET OUR STANDARDS SLIP. WE PRIDE OURSELVES, AT EAST MIDLANDS FREIGHT, IN THE FACT THAT, DESPITE ALL OUR PROBLEMS, WE SET OURSELVES VERY HIGH STANDARDS. WE MUST MAINTAIN THESE STANDARDS AT ALL COSTS.

Rumours have abounded in recent weeks that I am about to leave EMF as a result of the privatisation announcement. It is true that I can expect my time to be spent more and more on this work. Any manager might be called upon to be seconded to a part—time or full-time project team. However, I feel that my services are best placed by remaining here in Nottingham. I give you my commitment to working hard to ensure that the interests of all staff will be best protected as the proposals develop. I still believe, as strongly as ever, that there is a bright future for freight transportation by rail—both in this country and into Europe. I intend to work with this belief firmly in mind. Your management team shares my commitment to work towards the future. I hope you will continue to share it too.

Yours sincerely
Tim Edwards
Area Manager
East Midlands Freight

It was still 'business as usual' as, on 5 September 1993, Trainload Coal staged one of its most successful open days ever seen at Worksop, which was authorised by Kim Jordan. There were shuttle trains on what was termed Trainload Coal motive power day, and both to twin the depot with Trainload Freight and to mark the open day, 58011 was named *Worksop Depot* at the event by Doug Furniss, retired driver and open day secretary.

Mainline Freight

The year 1994 saw yet another re-organisation, with BR being split up into various parts with the aim of promoting competition between the businesses. The passenger side was split up into twenty-five shadow franchise train operating units (TOUs), split by geographical area and service type. On 9 June 1994, six freight operating companies (FOCs) were formed, of which three Trainload Freight units were also in geographical areas and named Trainload Freight South-East, Trainload Freight North-East, and Trainload Freight West.

With each company having a view of an annual turnover of around £150 million, they were allocated different areas, which varied in size. Trainload Freight South-East was responsible for freight operations in the south-east of England, East Anglia, the East Midlands, and parts of Warwickshire, Oxfordshire, Wiltshire, Somerset, and Avon. Trainload Freight North-East had the smallest geographical area, while Trainload Freight West encompassed the largest area, including all of Scotland, Wales, and the north-west of England.

The three were re-branded on 8 September 1994 as Mainline Freight, Loadhaul, and Transrail respectively. The other three FOCs were Railfreight Distribution, Freightliner, and Rail Express Systems.

Worksop came under the Mainline Freight banner with Kim Jordan as managing director and Tony Turton as regional manager for the east and Midlands. As the locos were also spilt between the companies, the Class 56s were transferred away to Loadhaul and Transrail, leaving Worksop with Classes 58 and 60 in the main, with the odd visiting Class 37.

The company introduced a livery of 'aircraft blue' with a silver bodyside stripe and 'rolling wheels' logo with 'Mainline' branding, although most locos retained the Trainload Freight two-tone grey livery with the addition of the Mainline Freight logo as an 'interim' livery. No. 58011 *Worksop Depot* displayed the interim livery at a launch event at its namesake depot on 14 November.

One of the downsides of the split was that Worksop men lost the Aire Valley power station traffic to Knottingley-based Loadhaul men. This also included traffic from the Shirebrook area pits.

In preparation for the 1993 Worksop open day, Class 26 D5300 was sent all the way from Eastfield depot. On 3 September 1993, D5300 heads a line-up of locomotives in Worksop Down side that were waiting to be placed in their final display position. No. 37692 *The Lass O Ballochmyle* is behind along with several other Trainload Coal-liveried locos.

Another two exhibits were sourced from Westbury by event organiser Barry Taylor; these were 59001 *Yeoman Endeavour* and 59102 *Village of Chantry*.

The logos for the new companies—Mainline, Loadhaul, and Transrail.

No. 56003 displays the Loadhaul livery to perfection while stabled in Worksop downside on a freezing 3 January 1997.

After bringing in a set of empty wagons to Worksop yard, instead of travelling back to Milford light engine and taking up a freight path, Loadhaul 56027 was attached to 58022, which was working 6R57 Worksop to Gascoigne Wood. The combination is seen departing Shireoaks East on 1 March 1995.

No. 56099 *Fiddlers Ferry Power Station* in Transrail 'Big T' livery heads a southbound loaded MGR working through the cutting at Barrow Hill for Ratcliffe on 22 March 1995. The partially filled cutting in the bottom right of the image was once a single line from Barrow Hill to Summit, on the route to Seymour Junction.

In its freshly applied Mainline livery, 60044 *Ailsa Craig* waits at Worksop West No. 23 signal with 7B62 Clipstone to West Burton on 7 June 1996.

For locos that had not received the blue livery, Mainline applied their 'rolling wheels' decals to the freight grey livery. Here, 60011 *Cader Idris* passes the site of Mansfield Concentration Sidings with 6Y31 Worksop to Bilsthorpe on 28 October 1995.

Transrail 60056 *William Beveridge* backs down the branch to Clipstone colliery with 6T65 from Thoresby on 15 January 1997.

English, Welsh, and Scottish Railways

The privatisation process carried on, and on 11 December 1995, the management of Mainline Freight, backed by Candover and Associated British Ports Holdings (ABPH), formed a bidding consortium for the three former Trainload Freight companies. ABPH confirmed that they were taking a 20 per cent equity stake in the bid by a consortium of trade and financial institutions led by Candover, together with the management and employees of Mainline Freight, to purchase the three operating units of Trainload Freight as part of the rail privatisation programme. ABPH believed that 'The Mainline Freight consortium can win new business from road to rail and will be well-placed to handle the bulk trades which move through the ports of ABPH and other UK seaports.'

However, the bid was unsuccessful, and on 24 February 1996, all three companies were acquired by 'North-South Railways', a company formed by a consortium led by US railroad company Wisconsin Central, for a combined total of £225.15 million. With the later addition of Rail Express Systems, the four companies initially continued to trade under their existing names, but on 25 April 1996, the new maroon and yellow corporate image of the owning company was unveiled—English, Welsh, and Scottish Railway (EW&S, later EWS).

The first loco to be seen in the new livery at Worksop was 58033, having travelled light engine from Doncaster on 21 May 1996. On this loco, the yellow band was high up, almost at cant rail level, and subsequent Class 58s were out-shopped with the yellow band midway along the bodyside.

The first of the class to receive EW&S livery was 58033, and it is seen here as it stands at Worksop West No. 21 signal with 7F87 Welbeck to Cottam on 2 July 1996.

Merry-Go-Round Wagons

Of course, the coal story was as much about the wagons themselves as the locos and operations. Worksop was a centre of operations for the pit-to-power station MGR services being introduced to the Trent Valley power stations, so in 1966, a new three-road wagon repair depot was constructed in the Down side yard. This was for servicing the two-axle wagons, initially classified as HOP32 AB, which had been the mainstay of MGR operations. From inception, more than 11,000 wagons would be built between 1965 and 1982.

With the introduction of the total operations processing system (TOPS) in 1973, the standard wagons were re-coded as HAA with a maximum speed of 45 mph loaded and 60 mph empty. The standard wagons were later followed by the HDA and HMA types with modified axle springs or modified brake actuators to allow for 60-mph operation when loaded, and the HCA and HFA types with canopies to reduce the amount of coal dust blowing off. The final development was the HBA, which was both canopied and capable of 60 mph when loaded.

By the turn of privatisation, consideration was given to increasing train loads. The standard set of MGR wagons ran to thirty-six, but although some locations could take forty-two wagons, it was not always possible to lengthen trains to any degree due to the constraints of the network of colliery run-round loops and sidings. Subsequently, the use of bogie hopper wagons was looked at, and on 14–15 September 1992, tests were carried out with two Tiphook bogie wagons in the consist of 7G14 on the 5.48 p.m. Harworth to Thorpe Marsh power station service, hauled by 58021. The use of the two wagons within the usual thirty-six-wagon set displaced four HAAs, making the train length no longer than the full set but with a tonnage increase from 130 tons (carried by the four displaced HAAs) to 200 tons carried by the two bogie wagons—a clear indication that bogie wagons were the way forward.

National Power was formed by the privatisation of the CEGB in 1990 and relied on coal deliveries by rail for its power stations. It was soon decided that it would be more cost-effective to use their own locomotives and wagons for these trains, and it was also decided that the trains of limestone required for the desulphurisation plants should also be moved in-house. Following the examples set by Foster Yeoman and ARC, who bought their own locomotives from General Motors Electro-Motive Division (59001-005 and 59101-104 respectively) and their own wagons, National Power did likewise, and 59201 was ordered for delivery in February 1994, together with twenty-one bogie hopper wagons to TOPS code JHA.

As the coal trials with the Tiphook hoppers had been successful, a further five locos (59202–206) were ordered along with a batch of eighty-five 100-ton bogie hopper coal wagons—initially also allocated TOPS code JHA but soon recoded to JMA. The first of the wagons were delivered in May 1995 with the locos following that August.

Based at a purpose-built depot at Ferrybridge, the National Power fleet with their striking blue and grey livery soon became a common sight around Gascoigne Wood, and from October 1995, they were seen being loaded at Maltby Colliery.

With the reduction in coal traffic, large numbers of wagons of all sorts had been withdrawn and stored or scrapped, and by the year 2000, the HAA and its derivatives had been reduced to around 4,500 wagons, which included the stored examples. With the fleet of National Power locos and wagons having been taken over by EWS in 1998, the bogie wagon proliferated when EWS introduced 1,144 bogie coal hoppers (coded HTA) between 2001 and 2004 for haulage behind their GM Class 66/0.

EWS's domination of the coal market was threatened when Freightliner (having primarily been concerned with its container and intermodal business) began its Heavy Haul operations in 1999, initially to move infrastructure trains for Railtrack and later Network Rail, eventually moving into the bulk sector. The company purchased their own 100-ton bogie hopper version, the HHA (later joined by the HXA, which was shorter but could carry the same payload, allowing an increase in tonnage hauled while keeping the train length the same) for haulage behind their GM Class 66/5 and Class 66/6. GB Railfreight (GBRf) also entered the market from 1999, initially for hauling infrastructure traffic but also with an eye on the bulk sector. Their striking blue and orange-liveried GM Class 66/7s were seen hauling another bogie hopper variant, the HYA (and later IIA), and by August 2010, the use of the four-wheel HAA wagons had ceased.

Of the 11,162 MGR hoppers built, at the time of writing, just seventeen examples of the HAA/HMA variants exist. However, a variant for moving China clay (the CDA) can still be seen in large numbers, some of which were converted from HAAs.

National Power 59201 *Vale of York* working as 6W32 Ferrybridge to Maltby arrives at Maltby on 29 October 1997. National Power was the first company to use bogie coal hoppers.

The horse seems disinterested in the 3,300-hp 66191 behind him. The loco is working the 6R14 1.49 p.m. Immingham to Drax at Knabbs Bridge near Melton Ross on 6 March 2007, the train comprising of twenty-one HTA hoppers, the second type of bogie coal hoppers introduced.

Passing Hasland near Chesterfield, Freightliner 66513 works the 4G48 10 a.m. Rugeley to Kellingley Colliery on 2 March 2007. The train is comprised of HHA hoppers, these being introduced in 2000.

GBRf 66719 sits on No. 1 road at Thoresby Colliery Junction on 11 June 2007. This was the first working by GBRf into Thoresby Colliery, with the train comprised of brand new HYA hoppers.

Completing the Worksop Depot Story

Although beyond the 1990s, the brief conclusion to the Worksop depot story is that Wisconsin Central, who had a 42.5-per cent stake in EWS, sold it to Canadian National in October 2001, although the EWS brand remained. On 13 November 2007, the German rail company Deutsche Bahn announced it had agreed to purchase EWS, and from then on, Worksop came under the DB Schenker banner, being rebranded as such from 1 January 2009. Due to changing coal patterns, the wagon repair depot was closed on 21 December 2009.

The last shift for ground staff based at Worksop was 23 July 2010, and the yards were only manned on an as-required basis from then on. With the announcement of the closure of the train crew depot in 2015, the final link was for the following thirty-three drivers: Dean Stewart, Ashley Torr, Lee Burnett, Paul Caley, Graham Ward, Chris Smith, Julian Farrell, Shaun Arum, Dave Cook, Laura Stannard (Worksop's only female driver), Anthony (Tony) Burniston, Paul Brammer, Dale Shipley, Richard Oakley, Nick Castings, Keith Gillett, Brian Smith, Bob Wigley, Shaun Arlis, Joe Harding, Rich Rodgers, Jonathan Jarman, Jonathan Shipman, Gary Whitehouse, Steve Coney, Phil Shooter, Kevin Johnson, Mick Yates, Barry Foster, John Davison, Paul Green, Ross Carline, and Paul Bullas.

These drivers had route knowledge that encompassed three routes to Immingham (via Scunthorpe, Brigg, and Lincoln), as far south as Birmingham, Ratcliffe power station, Peak Forest via Sheffield station and Knottingley and Milford to the north. Some drivers retained Leicester and certain Sandite workings. Nine left on 26 September—six under VRS conditions and three to other companies—and one more took retirement. A further eleven moved to Rotherham, two to Toton, one to Eastleigh, one to Immingham, and the remainder were split between Doncaster and Knottingley.

Worksop ASLEF branch No. 240, first established around 1920, closed in mid-October, and the depot closed at midnight on 31 October 2015, marking the end of an era.

The final word on the depot is that the end of December 2018 saw the majority of the freehold interest in Worksop wagon repair depot and the Down side yard bought by Harry Needle Railroad Company from DB Cargo UK, with plans to invest £6 million into the site. The remaining stored wagons were either cut up on site or moved away for cutting up. The final wagon to leave Worksop Down side was to be 310000, the first HTA to be built, which was claimed by the NRM.

New fencing and a gate across the yard throat were erected in February 2019, and trackwork repairs began in March 2019. The yard has now taken in its first trains of rolling stock for temporary or long-term store. The first to arrive was on 29 May 2019 when 37608 arrived from Old Dalby with Crossrail unit 345 023. This was followed on 4 June when 66749 brought in an ECML Mark 4 set from Bounds Green. There were further arrivals on 8 June with 66718 bringing in another Mark 4 set on 12 June with 37611 hauling 345 056 and on 17 June 37601 with 345 057.

Next to arrive was Crossrail 345 058 on 19 June, and on the same day, 47715 was brought in by rail, while 08904 was brought in by road, this 08 arriving almost ten years after 08633 left Worksop in December 2009. The 47 is used to keep the stored stock powered up, while the Class 08 was fitted with a Dellner coupler to allow it to move the new Crossrail stock. Since then, examples of classes 01, 08, 20, and 25 have been brought in for various reasons. Mid-2020 saw HNRC also take over the Up yard and trackwork repairs undertaken, with off-lease rolling stock coming in for storage.

Today, the yards are full again, but they have gone from coal wagons to coaching stock.

The final Class 08 diagram at Worksop was for the wagon repair depot and here after being stored inside the WRD over the weekend, 08633 is started up for its final days work at Worksop on 19 December 2009.

With driver John Shipman at the helm, 08633 performs the final shunts at Worksop wagon repair depot, the last weekend of an 08 at Worksop on 19 December 2009.

A far cry from the days of coal wagons in the down side yard at Worksop. With the purchase of the yard by Harry Needle, items of rolling stock are being brought in for storage. Here, the third East Coast Mk 4 set is being shunted into the yard, while 47715 is being used for powering up stored stock. In the background, 08904 waits its next duties, while a stored Elizabeth Line Class 345 unit waits it future.

2

Declining UK Coal Production

The year 1913 was the peak production of coal—287 million tons were produced, of which 30 per cent was exported, and demand was rising at 4 per cent per year. However, after the First World War, exports plummeted due to increased competition, while domestic demand remained stagnant. The deep coal-mining industry in Britain then began a slow decline, and there were significant colliery closures after the Second World War.

At the time of nationalisation of the coal industry in 1947, the NCB took over the running of 970 working pits, 120 of which were in the East Midlands region alone. The East Midlands formed just a part of the Derbyshire, Nottinghamshire, and Yorkshire coalfield, with mining concentrated into three different regions—the Leicestershire and South Derbyshire coalfield, the North Derbyshire coalfield, and the Nottinghamshire coalfield, which stretched along the western fringe of the county from Nottingham to Worksop. The South Yorkshire coalfield covered most of South Yorkshire, West Yorkshire, and a small part of North Yorkshire.

In 1952, the coal industry produced 228 million tons, 95 per cent of which was from deep mines and the remainder from opencast sites. The Clean Air Act of 1956 saw a turn towards more modern forms of central heating, with rail transport also moving towards diesel and electric power. By 1960, around 600 collieries were still producing coal, but this had halved to around 300 by 1970. There was a ten-week walkout in 1972, which saw electricity blackouts and the instigation of a three-day week, and then in 1974, a further dispute resulted in no production for four weeks.

There was a worldwide glut of coal in the period 1980–81, which meant that the British Coal industry and other coal-producing nations had a surplus. This made the lure of cheap, imported coal attractive to the NCB's customers, and in March 1984, Ian MacGregor, the NCB chairman, asked his area directors to reduce output by a total of 4 million tons nationally. The easiest way to achieve this was to close pits without the traditional consultation with the National Union of Mineworkers, and the choice of Cortonwood in Yorkshire, Polmaise in Scotland, and Snowdown Colliery in Kent would spark the bitter 1984–85 miners' strike.

The beginning of the strike saw just over 170 collieries in production in Britain, but the number of working collieries countrywide declined quickly between 1980 and 2000 as shown in Table 1.

Table 1: Working Collieries, 1980–2000			
Year	No. of Collieries	No. of Employees	UK Output in Tons (including opencast)
1980	211	230,000	127,000,000
1985	133	138,000	105,000,000
1990	65	57,000	92,000,000
1995	65	15,000	51,000,000
2000	28	8,000	31,000,000

By 1987, 10 million tons of coal was being imported, more than 60 per cent of which was from Australia and the USA. This led to people questioning why coal from such a distance could possibly be cheaper than home-produced coal. At the same time, natural gas was becoming ever more popular for power generation, and with the so-called 'Dash for Gas' leading to the privatisation of the electricity industry, further markets were lost.

Between 1990 and 1995, the production of coal almost halved from the same number of collieries with a large reduction in the workforce, but the last five years of the decade saw further reductions in output, collieries, and staff. Table 2 shows the East Midlands collieries and their outputs as served by Barrow Hill, Shirebrook, Toton, and Worksop men in 1990.

Table 2: East Midlands Collieries, 1990		
Colliery	Annual Output (Tonnes)	Average Trains Per Day
Worksop Area		
Harworth	1,400,000	4
Manton	1,125,000	4
Maltby	1,100,000	4
Kiveton Park	550,000	1
Thurcroft	500,000	1
Barrow Hill Area		
Markham	1,600,000	10
Oxcroft	750,000	2
Bolsover	650,000	3
Toton Area		
Bentinck	1,350,000	5
Cotgrave	900,000	3
Silverhill	850,000	3
Calverton	800,000	2
Gedling	600,000	2

Shirebrook Area		
Thoresby	2,300,000	8
Shirebrook	1,700,000	8
Ollerton	1,350,000	5
Welbeck	1,280,000	6
Bevercotes	1,250,000	3
Bilsthorpe	1,200,000	1
Clipstone	950,000	5
Sherwood	950,000	3
Rufford	900,000	2
Creswell	750,000	3
Source: Rail, February 1991		

On 13 October 1992, British Coal announced the closure of a further thirty-one pits nationwide, ten of which were to close immediately. It was suggested that as a result, it could cost BR in the region of £200 million, and up to 5,000 railway employees could lose their jobs, not to mention the almost 25,000 miners who would be out of work. In response to the huge public opinion, on 19 October, the government announced a moratorium to allow more time to consider the implications of the closure plan, although the general feeling was that this was merely a delaying tactic.

In the north-east, Easington, Vane Tempest/Seaham, Westoe, and Wearmouth were to go, and as they all relied on Sunderland South Dock depot for the movement of their coal, the eight Class 56s based there would have no work. In Yorkshire, eleven

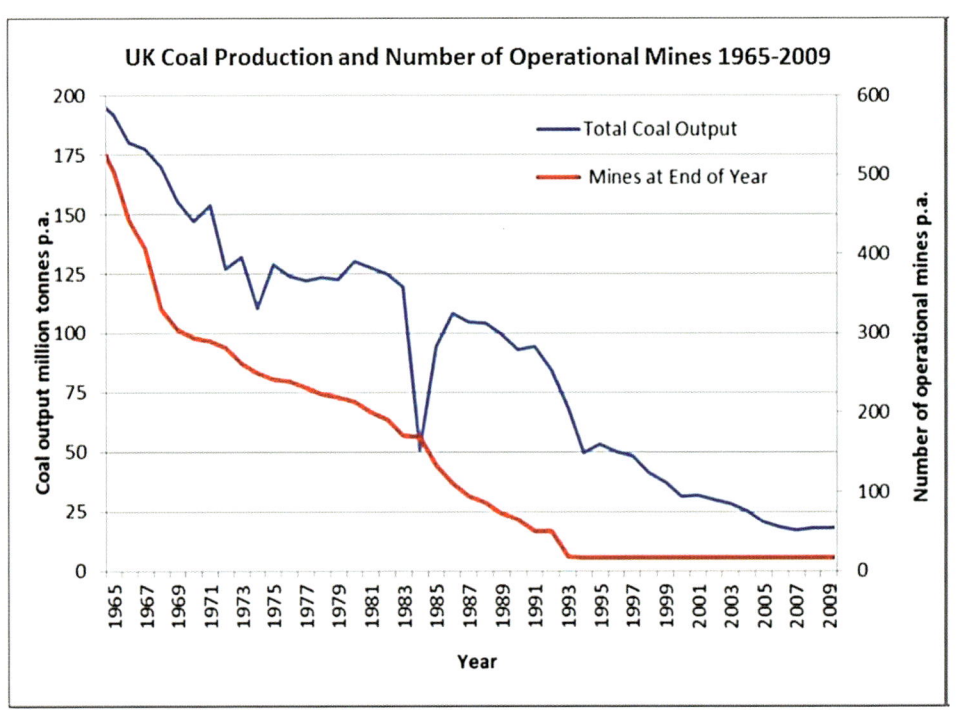

mines would be closed by March 1993, Doncaster being the hardest depot to be hit. Sharlston, Bentley, Markham Main, Rossington, and Thorne/Hatfield provided the majority of work for Doncaster Carr loco, and it was such that Knottingley depot could easily cope with the remaining traffic.

Elsewhere in Yorkshire, Frickley, Grimethorpe, Houghton Main, Kiveton Park, Prince of Wales, and Maltby were candidates for closure. Amazingly, the NCB defined their Midlands area to include the north-west of England, Derbyshire, and South Wales. Derbyshire would see the closure of Bolsover, Markham and Shirebrook, the north-west, Parkside, Point of Ayr, Silverdale, and Trentham. South Wales would see Betws Drift and Taff Merthyr go.

Nottinghamshire would lose Bevercotes, Calverton, Cotgrave, and Silverhill, together with their serving branch lines. Rufford and Bilsthorpe would close (and their branches) along with Clipstone, however the latter would re-open under privatisation thus also saving a small section of the former Mansfield Railway.

The loss of 59 miles of freight-only railway that served the closed mines would have been a big blow to Trainload Coal as this would also see a reduction of around sixty-three daily MGR services. The knock-on effect would be a loss of work for around thirty locos and their crews, and in places such as Sunderland South Dock, the reasons for their existence would vanish.

It was expected that manpower, depots, and routes would all be affected, and that redundancies in signalling and the support side of Trainload Coal would be a consequence. Trainload Coal had offices in Wales, Nottinghamshire, and the north-east, but with the reduction in traffic, it was felt that just one office would suffice, with management redundancies being a result.

With the passing of the Coal Industry Act 1994, just seven East Midlands collieries—all of them in Nottinghamshire—remained active, and mining operations were taken over by RJB Mining (named after owner Richard J. Budge) who ran most of the newly-privatised industry from 1995 until 2001, when Budge stood down as CEO of RJB Mining and UK Coal took over. Production continued in a downward spiral as markets for the coal gradually disappeared, and imported coal through the likes of Immingham and Hull docks took its place. Table 3 shows the declining output for Nottinghamshire coal as an example.

Table 3: Nottinghamshire Coal Output		
Year	Million Tonnes	
1995	8,230,000	
1996	8,320,000	
1997	7,700,000	
1998	6,270,000	
1999	6,160,000	
Annual Output for RJB Mining in 1996		
Colliery	Output	Men
Bilsthorpe	1,621,000	386
Clipstone	487,940	304
Thoresby	1,902,000	702
Welbeck	1,880,000	659

With the colliery undergoing demolition behind, 58019 *Shirebrook Colliery* is leaving Kiveton Colliery on the last Friday of trains from here, 12 May 1995.

Manton Colliery undergoing demolition in 1995.

By 1998, fifty-five collieries had closed, most of them being hastily capped off and swiftly demolished. Following their closure, some collieries still had stockpiles to be removed prior to final site clearance, and movement of these stockpiles by rail provided something of a swansong.

In the East Midlands area, the colliery closures had left Welbeck, Thoresby, and Clipstone to continue primarily serving the power stations at High Marnham, West Burton, Cottam, Ratcliffe, Drakelow, and Rugeley, with the occasional Didcot traffic from Welbeck. The weekly timetable of trains would vary considerably, depending on the power stations' demand for coal. A typical week in early 1998 looked something like Table 4.

Table 4: Coal Traffic from Worksop: Typical Week in January 1998					
Trains for High Marnham (HM)					
Code	Depart	Origin	Destination	Arrive	Runs
6K22	04.30	Worksop	Thoresby	05.26	SX
7J22	06.21	Thoresby	HM	08.15	SX
6K24	09.45	HM	Thoresby	11.26	SX
7J24	12.21	Thoresby	HM	13.30	SX
6K26	15.56	HM	Thoresby	17.26	SX
7J26	18.21	Thoresby	HM	19.26	SX
6W26	20.56	HM	Worksop	21.26	SX
6K27	07.30	Worksop	Thoresby	08.26	SX
7J27	09.21	Thoresby	HM	10.26	SX
6W27	12.50	HM	Worksop	13.40	SX
6K23	08.21	Worksop	Welbeck	09.15	SX
7J23	10.10	Welbeck	HM	10.50	SX
6K25	13.35	HM	Welbeck	14.35	MO
7J25	15.30	Welbeck	HM	16.40	MO
6K25	13.35	HM	Thoresby	14.26	MSX
7J25	15.21	Thoresby	HM	16.40	MSX
6W26	19.00	HM	Worksop	19.50	SX
Trains for West Burton					
7B58	03.21	Thoresby	West Burton	06.55	EWD
6K61	05.41	Worksop	Welbeck	06.35	MWO
7B61	07.30	Welbeck	West Burton	10.10	MWO
6K68	09.48	Worksop	Clipstone	10.34	MTWO
7B60	12.16	Clipstone	West Burton	17.05	MTWO
6K71	12.48	Worksop	Clipstone	13.34	MO
7B71	15.16	Clipstone	West Burton	20.20	MO
6K51	19.30	Worksop	Thoresby	20.26	SunTO
7B51	21.21	Thoresby	West Burton	23.59	SunTO
6K53	21.41	Worksop	Welbeck	22.35	SunTO
7B53	23.30	Welbeck	West Burton	02.10	SunTO

Trains for Cottam					
6K87	05.51	Worksop	Welbeck	06.35	TTHO
7F87	07.30	Welbeck	Cottam	12.25	TTHO
6K93	13.41	Worksop	Welbeck	14.35	TTHO
7F93	15.30	Welbeck	Cottam	18.05	TTHO
6K98	19.01	Worksop	Welbeck	19.55	SX
7F98	20.50	Welbeck	Cottam	23.00	SX
Trains for Ratcliffe					
6T14	06.49	Worksop	Clipstone	07.34	MWFO
7A14	09.16	Clipstone	Toton	13.30	MWFO
Trains for Drakelow					
6T46	03.01	Worksop	Welbeck	03.55	SX
7C46	04.50	Welbeck	Drakelow	08.30	SX
6T50	11.01	Worksop	Welbeck	11.55	MSX
7C50	12.50	Welbeck	Drakelow	16.30	MSX
Trains for Rugeley					
6T33	23.25	Toton	Welbeck	01.15	SunFX
7G33	02.10	Welbeck	Toton	04.00	SunFX

SX = Saturdays Excepted
EWD = Each Weekday
MO – Mondays Only
MWO = Monday Wednesday Only
MWFO = Monday Wednesday Friday Only
MTWO = Monday Tuesday Wednesday Only
MSX = Monday Saturday Excepted
TTHO = Tuesday Thursday Only
SunTO = Sunday Tuesday Only
SunFX = Sunday Friday Excepted

Opencast Coal

The National Coal Board was given responsibility for opencast coal production in 1952, when the Opencast executive was formed. In opencast mining, whole landscapes are dug out, but in the early years, the limitations of excavating plant saw surface mining restricted to depths of around 10 m (approx. 33 feet). By 1948, increases in plant size had allowed depths of 30 m (approx. 100 feet) to be obtained. By the 1990s, depths of 80 m (262 feet) were common. The deepest excavation at that time was 215 m (705 feet) at the former Westfield site in Scotland.

Opencast coal production had gone from a figure of 8 million tons in 1945 to 14 million tons in 1958, then dropped to 6.5 million tons in 1968. The 1970s saw demand improve, reaching 9.1 million tons by 1975–76 and 15 million tons in 1980–81. Output tripled after 1985, and by 1998, it accounted for one-third of coal production, the coal extracted this way being on average cheaper to produce than deep mined coal.

Opencast mining in operation. This was part of the Pithouse West opencast site, which saw an area of land between the Sheffield to Worksop railway and the Rother Valley country park dug out. This also encompassed the route of the Waleswood curve between the Great Central Main Line at Killamarsh and the Sheffield–Worksop line at Waleswood, which had closed in 1966 and had been buried beneath previous opencast working spoil heaps. The dumper truck is standing on the coal seam that was found, but also during excavation works, the former Waleswood Tunnel mouth was uncovered and can be seen high up on the side of the excavation. (*Courtesy of J. Batterham*)

The coal being mined was of good quality as the method of extraction ensured only clean coal was obtained, whereas underground conditions made it difficult to produce coal without taking some of the neighbouring rock strata as well. Opencast mining produced a blend of coal with good sizing qualities that could be transported by road to a disposal point, where it could be taken away by rail straight to the customer, or for further blended with other coal. In most opencast sites, 80 per cent was destined for power generation with the remainder shared between industrial and domestic use.

Oxcroft Opencast disposal point was the closest to Worksop and saw much activity from its opening. Table 5 shows a typical week's output from Oxcroft in 1998—the West Burton and Cottam traffic was worked by Worksop drivers and the Ratcliffe traffic by Toton drivers.

Table 5: Typical Week Coal Departures for Oxcroft (Week Commencing 13 September 1998)					
Code	Depart	Origin	Destination	Arrive	Runs
6K85	05.04	Worksop	Oxcroft	06.10	TFO
7F85	07.00	Oxcroft	Cottam	10.38	TFO
6K90	09.04	Worksop	Oxcroft	10.10	MO
6T14	08.30	Toton	Oxcroft	09.40	TTHO
7A14	10.30	Oxcroft	Ratcliffe	13.30	TTHO
6T17	11.00	Toton	Oxcroft	12.10	SX
7A17	13.00	Oxcroft	Ratcliffe	16.30	SX
7F90	11.00	Oxcroft	Cottam	15.00	MO

6K33	10.58	Worksop	Oxcroft	12.01	SX
7B33	13.00	Oxcroft	West Burton	15.52	SX
6K93	12.38	Worksop	Oxcroft	14.00	SX
7F32	15.00	Oxcroft	Cottam	18.15	SX

This disposal point was located in Stanfree, Derbyshire, just south of Clowne near the M1. Its main function was to process coal from opencast mining in the immediate area, commencing sending trainloads out in January 1980. Oxcroft Colliery No. 1 survived until 27 February 1976 and Oxcroft Colliery No. 5, a short-lived drift mine on the site of what would become Oxcroft Colliery No. 1 railway sidings, later became the Oxcroft coal disposal point.

The junction for the disposal point was on the former MR Clowne branch, which ran from Seymour Junction, on the Doe Lea Valley line, to Creswell Junction, immediately north of Elmton and Creswell on the Nottingham to Worksop line. Originally accessed via a ground frame on the Clowne branch, following closure of this line onwards to Creswell, the 1-mile line between Seymour Junction and Oxcroft Junction remained open to serve the disposal point, a staff being collected from Seymour Junction box by each train into the plant.

The branch passed beneath the B6419 Bolsover Road followed by the M1 motorway, and on entering the site, it separated into three sidings. After arrival in one of the sidings, the loco would detach from its empties and run around to collect an awaiting loaded set. The operation at Oxcroft was complicated by the steep gradient and the limited headshunt up to Mill Lane, which bordered the south side of the site. Consequently, incoming trains of HAAs or similar had to be broken into sets of four or five wagons, and the internal shunting loco would haul them up to Mill Lane and propel them down under the loader.

After seeing an image printed in *Rail* magazine, I decided that I should make the effort to visit the area, and my first photo taken at Oxcroft was of 58005 working 7C67 Oxcroft to Drakelow on 3 December 1993. This was taken as the train was

A tablet for the Seymour Junction to the Elmton and Creswell branch. The area around the wording 'Elmton & Creswell' has been ground out as it would originally have said Oxcroft Colliery Sidings No. 3, this being the next box along the line before closure in November 1969.

The Tyers Tablet machine, which dispensed tablets for the Seymour Junction to Elmton and Creswell branch, by this time out of use. On top are the staff for the Seymour Junction to Oxcroft section, which was used for each train, along with the Annett's key for the ground frames at Oxcroft Colliery Junction (curved top) and Bolsover Coalite branch (square top).

leaving Oxcroft and entailed climbing up the M1 motorway embankment to get the train as it approached the bridge beneath the motorway. Needless to say, I ensured I could not be seen from passing vehicles; it would not have done to find the motorway police breathing down my neck.

With the site being an easy drive from home, I visited many times over the years, even managing to gain entry and have a ride on the internal Hunslet loco not long before closure. This was Hunslet Works No. 8979 of 1979, a 0-6-0 Diesel Hydraulic with Rolls-Royce engine, twin-disc torque converter, and Hunslet final drive gearbox. Ex-BR Class 03 03037 had been used as an internal shunter at the site, arriving in February 1989 before being sold into preservation in 1995.

As the site lasted into the twenty-first century, I have many photos, but only those taken in the 1990s will be featured in this book. The disposal point closed in 2006 and was mothballed awaiting any future developments of opencast mining in the north-east Derbyshire coalfield area. There was a brief reprieve in 2007 when UK Coal started a coal recovery operation to sift through nearby pit tips and recovered around 14,000 tons of coal before the site was again mothballed. Permission for the coal-stocking expired in 2009, and Derbyshire County Council refused planning permission to extend the licence for the site in 2010. Track was stolen from the site, and eventually, all the buildings were demolished and the site has since been partly restored to nature.

No. 58006 is seen leaving Oxcroft disposal point with 7C75 to Drakelow 'C' power station on 17 March 1994.

No. 60011 *Cader Idris* has just taken the line for Oxcroft at Seymour on 29 March 1995. The line to Elmton and Creswell via Clowne is in the foreground, this being out of use at the time. The Oxcroft branch was worked with a staff obtained at Seymour Junction box, while the Elmton and Creswell branch was worked by a tablet.

No. 60011 now curves off away from the Clowne branch and heads towards the disposal point on 29 March 1995.

No. 60011 is now about to pass beneath the B6419 Bolsover Road.

No. 03037 is seen acting as the internal shunter at Oxcroft disposal point on 3 December 1993. New to 32A (Norwich) on 9 February 1959, it was withdrawn from there on 29 September 1976. Sold into industry in 1977, it arrived at Oxcroft Opencast disposal point on 2 February 1989. It was sold into preservation in 1995.

No. 56131 *Ellington Colliery* at Oxcroft disposal point running around its train to make 7F35 for Ferrybridge on 17 November 1995. On the left are two industrial shunters then out of use, while behind the Class 56 is Hunslet Works No. 8979 of 1979 in use for shunting the wagons.

No. 66017 is seen while the train preparers are getting the train ready to depart from Oxcroft with MEAs forming 6G47 for Doncaster Decoy on 1 May 1999.

After being prepared, 66017 is now departing from Oxcroft and heading towards the bridge beneath the M1 Motorway with MEAs forming 6G47 for Doncaster Decoy on 1 May 1999.

3
Nottinghamshire Area Collieries

Following on from Worksop depot and the decline of coal, we will now go back to the very beginning and the reason I began to write the book in the first place—to showcase the colliery and power stations photos I took back in the 1990s. We begin by examining the Nottinghamshire area pits I photographed, most of which were still open at my first visit, but closures would see them off one at a time. There will be a brief history of each colliery and then the photos I took at the time I was there.

Bentinck

Owned by the New Hucknall Colliery Company, three shafts were sunk, and production commenced at Bentinck Colliery in 1896. The pit was named after Cavendish-Bentinck, a surname associated with the dukes of Portland and their descendants.

Bentinck was originally served by connections from the ex-Great Central Railway (GCR) Chesterfield loop line either side of Kirkby Bentinck station, from the ex-Midland Railway's Pye Bridge to Kirkby line (diverging at Bentinck Colliery sidings signal box), and from the line that also served Langton Colliery (closed in 1966). The latter line was also connected to the Pye Bridge line and was controlled by Pinxton signal box.

In 1982, Bentinck amalgamated with nearby Annesley to form the Annesley-Bentinck concentration scheme, which saw all coal from Annesley, Bentinck, and Newstead being sent, via an incline drift, to the surface preparation plant at Bentinck. Men and materials were sent down via Annesley's shafts; this gave Bentinck the largest surface coal preparation plant in Europe. Bentinck retained its railway connection at Pinxton, whereas all the other connections and the line to Annesley were dismantled, with most of the output from Bentinck then going to Ratcliffe power station.

Nottinghamshire Area Collieries

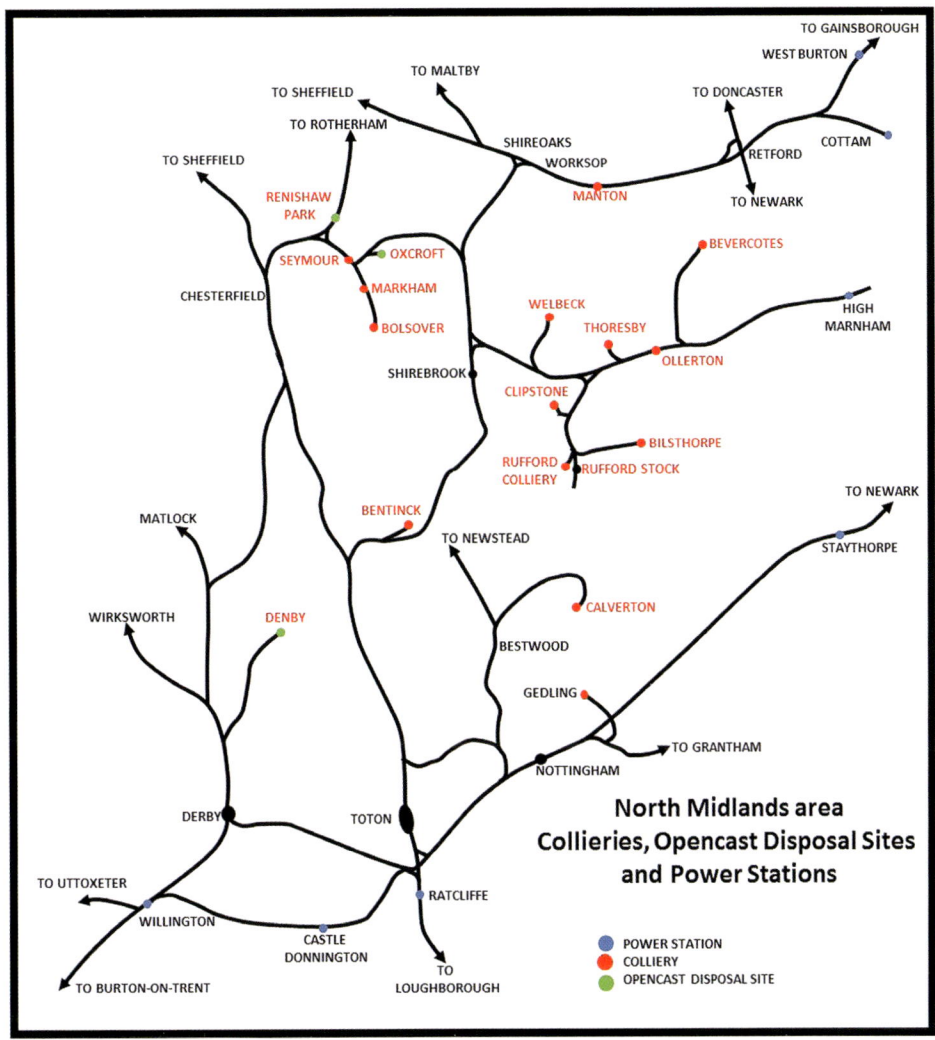

Map showing the location of collieries, opencast disposal points, and power stations in the North Midlands mentioned in the book.

With four exits from the mine (three shafts and a drift), it was said to be the safest pit at which to work if anything happened below ground, on account of the multiple exits. Bentinck's No. 1 shaft was sealed in December 1988, No. 3 shaft followed in August 1990, and the final shaft (No. 2) was filled in December 1992.

My first visit to the Pinxton area was on 9 February 1994. I parked in Pinxton and consulted an ordnance survey map to find the required location. This entailed a walk beneath the M1 motorway via an underbridge (built for the long-closed Pinxton Colliery to Langton Colliery branch), along the embankment paralleling the Pye Bridge line bridge, climbed the motorway embankment, and used that to cross the railway to the other side, ensuring I remained unseen by staying below the level of the motorway crash barriers.

At this point, the Bentinck branch curved in and paralleled the main line beneath the M1 as far as Langton Junction, where it connected to the Pye Bridge line. I photographed 58007 there as it trundled towards the end of the branch with 7A30 Bentinck to Ratcliffe power station. I returned to this location a few times over the years, but the first photos taken at the colliery itself were of 58026 *Drakelow Power Station* loading 7A30 for Ratcliffe on 11 February 1994.

As privatisation of the coal industry reached its climax, Bentinck became the last colliery to be sold by British Coal, becoming the property of Coal Investments. The first train to leave the colliery under this tenure was on 31 May 1995 when 58002 hauled 7A04 for Ratcliffe.

Unfortunately, Coal Investments went bankrupt in 1996, and Midlands Mining was set up by four directors of the pit with the aid of venture capitalists. The pit carried on sending out its products, but in January 1999, it was announced that Midlands Mining was intending to close Annesley-Bentinck colliery by the end of the year, due to geological problems and adverse market conditions.

With that news, Bentinck became a regular haunt for photographers and my last visit was to be on 2 November 1999.

Viewed from the M1 Motorway embankment on a murky 9 February 1994, 58007 *Drakelow Power Station* reaches the end of the Bentinck branch with 7A30 Bentinck to Ratcliffe. The line between Pye Bridge and Kirkby is in the foreground, the colliery is on the extreme right horizon.

My first actual colliery shot at Bentinck was a close up of the loading bunker taken through the fence adjacent to Mill Lane as 58007 *Drakelow Power Station* makes its way through the typical filth of a pit yard. It is loading 7A30 for Ratcliffe at Bentinck on 11 February 1994.

I had seen a shot published in *Rail* magazine taken from the hillside overlooking the colliery by prolific photographer Dave Peachy and decided to take a similar photo. So again, armed with an OS map, I reconnoitred the area and eventually found the location, which was through a field alongside Mill Lane. Here is the photo I got that day, on 8 June 1994; in the foreground is the Pye Bridge to Kirkby line, just above which is Mill Lane. In the colliery, 58027 is loading 7G61 to take to Rufford Stocking Site with coal for blending.

Zooming in to the colliery, here is a closer shot of 7A04 being loaded with 58002 *Daw Mill Colliery* at the head on 31 May 1995.

Another day, another train, and here, 58004 arrives at Bentinck on 27 April 1999 with 6T21 ex-Toton, once again as viewed from the top of the hill opposite the colliery.

After taking the shot from the hillside, it was a mad dash down to find another spot to photograph the train, and here is the result. No. 58004 now backs out of the bunker as it is loaded at Bentinck to form 7A21 for Ratcliffe on 27 April 1999.

No. 58032 *Thoresby Colliery* is ready to depart from Bentinck and is seen from the access road to Meadow Farm, with 7A21 on the 6 p.m. departure for Ratcliffe on 28 April 1999.

Glorious evening light illuminates 58004 as it ambles down the Bentinck branch at Langton Hall with 7A21 on the 6 p.m. departure for Ratcliffe power station on 27 April 1999.

Above left: Loadhaul livery 56077 *Thorpe Marsh Power Station* working 7A21 on the 6 p.m. departure from Bentinck to Ratcliffe passes Langton Hall with Bentinck colliery on the horizon on 26 July 1999.

Above right: Back in Trainload Coal days, 56006 leaves the Bentinck branch with 7A25 Bentinck to Ratcliffe as 58021 approaches on the main line with 7V06 from Welbeck to Didcot on 17 March 1994.

Bevercotes

This was the newest colliery of the North Nottinghamshire Area, the sinking of which did not commence until 1954. It was sunk as part of the post-war expansion of the coal industry and was intended to be one of the pits tapping into the previously untouched deeper coal. Hailed as the first 'push-button' colliery in the world, it had an underground control centre to monitor production and tower-mounted Koepe winders or Friction winding type. This uses a single loop of wire rope, or two or more ropes in parallel, and a powered pulley or 'Koepe' wheel to wind rather than the standard drum. The system was invented in Germany in 1877 by Frederick Koepe (pronounced 'Cope'), the first British example being installed at Bestwood Colliery in the 1880s.

The colliery was to be one of the 'state of the art' mines of the modern NCB, but when opening day approached, underground development was struggling and none of the faces were yet ready to turn coal. Embarrassingly, coal had to be brought from Ollerton pit and run into Bevercotes, just to show something coming out on the belts for the press and officials.

Surface facilities included modern pit head baths, large workshops and a huge coal preparation plant, along with a fan of empty and loaded sidings. These facilities included a Carriage & Wagon (C&W) repair siding, cabin and workshop, and also a locomotive turntable.

Rail access to the colliery was via a new 4.5-mile-long single-track branch from Boughton Junction (on the Shirebrook to High Marnham line), construction of the branch entailing a large amount of earthworks and new bridges—half being on embankment, the rest in cutting. There was signalling at the Bevercotes end of the single line, two concrete huts being provided near the River Meden Bridge—one was the 'signalling hut', the other a permanent way cabin.

Production problems persisted at Bevercotes, and when the headings team found coal, it was not followed for long before a fault line was hit, where the strata had sheared vertically—the colliery having been sunk in an area of significant faulting. Further attempts at production were eventually abandoned, and the mine was partially mothballed while further extensive development work took place, in an attempt to go beyond the faulted areas. During this time, the railway facilities were also mothballed.

When thoughts at Bevercotes turned finally to starting serious production, a modernisation of the 'modern' facilities was deemed necessary, part of which included the construction of an ultra-modern rapid-loading bunker. The existing sidings were lifted and a brand-new line was laid, with a run-round and cripple wagon siding, in what became the standard NCB rapid-loading layout. Unlike later facilities that used Toton signals (an indicator signal for controlling loading or unloading movements first used in Toton Marshalling Yard), three-aspect colour light signals initially controlled trains leaving the bunker. These gave indications to the driver as follows:

Green:	Draw forward at 0.5 mph
Yellow:	Prepare to stop
Red:	Stop immediately
Red with Flashing Yellow:	Reverse until yellow flashing light is extinguished.

Toton signals at Thoresby Colliery. The three flashing white lights at 45 degrees means 'move slowly in the opposite direction to that required for loading or unloading'.

Bevercotes would never be a very productive pit; indeed, there were some weeks where more oil was produced than coal, as the North Nott's oil field was located in the same area with the oil measures laying close to the coal, and as a result, the oil would seep into the workings. Hope of expansion into mega production never happened, and the requirement to have two trains at the pit at the same time did not occur. As such, BR abolished the colour light signalling method, and Toton Signals were eventually provided, the branch then becoming one train working until the end. The colliery was mothballed in 1993 with the final trains serving the Bolsover Coalite plant with a 12.30 a.m. departure, which I photographed twice, the better one being on 13 May 1993.

Bevercotes closed in September 1993, but after demolition and site clearance, there was still 360,000 tons of stockpiled coal remaining. On 22 November 1996, 58023 ran a series of light engine proving runs along the branch prior to the resumption of trains to clear this coal, and the following day, a new short-term traffic flow commenced, bringing coal from Asfordby mine in Leicestershire to be blended with the stockpile. Running as 6Z68 Asfordby to Bevercotes and headed by 58015, being 'in the know', I managed to photograph the train at Bevercotes and get chatting with the ground staff. A few days later, a pair of Class 37s was diagrammed to work the train, but in those early internet days, there were very few that knew about it.

After blending, the coal was taken forward to High Marnham power station. The first such train ran as 7J23 on 25 November 1996, but after two-thirds of the consist had been loaded, the coal was deemed too wet and High Marnham subsequently refused to take the train. Consequently, after loading had finished, the train ran

The first image I ever had published was this one of 56018 under the bunker lights at Bevercotes Colliery, while loading 7Z27 on the 12.30 a.m. Bevercotes to Bolsover Coalite. This was taken just after midnight on 13 May 1993 with an exposure of 15 sec at F8—the things we do for photos.

No. 58015 unloading 6Z68 Asfordby to Bevercotes, the first train of coal for blending with the closed Bevercotes colliery stockpile on 23 November 1996.

After two trains had run in with coal for blending, it was time to send out the blended coal. Here on 25 November 1996, EWS red livery 58033 is loading 7J23 for High Marnham, this being the first train out of the colliery stockpile.

The loaded train was refused by High Marnham, and as such, it went to Worksop instead. Here 58033 travels along the Bevercotes branch at Boughton on 25 November 1996.

More interesting traction was utilised on the train from Asfordby on 21 December 1996. Here, 37694 and 37884 are seen unloading 6Z68 ex-Asfordby.

Mainline blue-liveried 58038 is seen at Haughton with 6K90 Worksop to Bevercotes on 19 March 1997.

around at Boughton Junction and went to Worksop, then later to Rufford stocking site for further blending.

I would return several times to photograph trains along the Bevercotes branch while the stockpiled coal was being removed, but after their cessation in 1997, nothing else has used the branch since and although there were plans to include the line in a Network Rail test facility, nothing came of it and the track has been lifted.

Bilsthorpe

Bilsthorpe Colliery was owned by the Stanton Ironworks Company Ltd, and the colliery branch opened in January 1925 to allow construction traffic to the pit, with shaft-sinking beginning in July 1925. The branch was initially a temporary line, and diverged from the Rufford branch at Bilsthorpe Colliery Junction, 1 mile 396 yards from Rufford Junction.

Production commenced in August 1927 when the top hard seam was reached by shafts 482 yards deep. The colliery branch was made permanent early in 1928 when shaft-sinking had been completed.

The branches to Rufford and Bilsthorpe were originally worked by key token operation. At the divergence of the Bilsthorpe line from the Rufford Colliery branch, a new signal box known as Rufford Branch signal box was opened in 1927. It was, however, short-lived and closed on 12 July 1931. It was officially abolished on 24 February 1932, to be replaced with a two-lever ground frame.

On 19 October 1975, Bilsthorpe Colliery sidings were remodelled, but on Sunday, 4 January 1976, all sidings in the colliery area were taken out of use pending removal when rapid-loading facilities were commissioned, and the single line was then connected into a new layout.

On 23 April 1989, I made my first visit. Although just out of the timescale of this book, it is included for interest. On that day, the Institution of Mining Engineers ran the Notts and North Derbyshire rail tour to several collieries. Originating at Derby, the rail tour visited Bentinck, Welbeck, Bilsthorpe, Blidworth, Rufford, Thoresby, Bevercotes, Warsop, Markham, Sutton, and Silverhill collieries. The DMU stock used for the rail tour was allocated to Tyseley and was formed by T227 (54027 and 53019), T319 (51129, 59756, and 51149), and T303 (51406, 59516, and 51364). As I was roped in to help Worksop-based area inspector Brian Bates with clipping the points in the collieries, it placed me in a fortunate position to photograph the train in several locations.

Photographs of the colliery on normal visits were available from Eakring Road overbridge, but on two occasions, I was granted permission by the colliery manager to photograph from the far end of the bunker line. Usually, the train loco was at the leading end of the incoming empties as it passed beneath the bunker, then during loading, propelled back to the other side of the road bridge to access the run-round loop. However, for a period, trains were top and tailed due to a derailment in the loop, thus allowing a photo of the loco at the rear of the train.

Above left: No. 60069 *Humphrey Davy* is seen at it passes the run-round loop on the approach to Bilsthorpe with 6V06 from Toton on a wet 29 September 1993.

Above right: Due to derailment in the run-round loop at Bilsthorpe trains were top and tailed for a period and here 58020 *Doncaster Works* is seen at the rear of 7A07 on the 4.40 p.m. Bilsthorpe to Ratcliffe on 13 April 1995. One of the errant wagons is parked in the cripple siding awaiting later collection.

With 58020 now out of view, 58013 (which was the engine that brought the train in) is now at the rear of 7A07 on the 4.40 p.m. Bilsthorpe to Ratcliffe, as it is hauled away from Bilsthorpe to head to Thoresby to run around.

Granted permission to photograph from 'inside the fence', here 56100 is arriving at Bilsthorpe to load 7C10 for Eggborough on 14 June 1995. No. 58028 was at the other end and would lead the ensemble to Thoresby where the train would reverse and head towards Shirebrook.

Here is 58028 at the rear of 7C10 while loading at Bilsthorpe during the top and tailing period on 14 June 1995.

No. 58046 *Asfordby Mine* in Mainline Blue livery arrives at Bilsthorpe with 6K27 from Worksop on 27 March 1997, the day after cutting of coal ceased at the colliery.

With the headstocks of Clipstone Colliery on the horizon, 58045 passes Rufford Junction with 6K24 High Marnham to Bilsthorpe Colliery on 27 March 1997. This junction was installed between the former Midland Railway Clipstone branch and the former GCR Rufford branch and opened on 12 December 1983. The line in the foreground is to Rufford Colliery, and the train is on the former GCR side, the grassed area is the former MR line towards Clipstone.

No. 58040 *Cottam Power Station* comes off the Bilsthorpe branch with 7F98 Bilsthorpe Colliery to Cottam, the last train to be loaded at Bilsthorpe and use the branch on 29 April 1997. The tin hut once contained at key token machine for the section from Rufford Junction to Bilsthorpe Junction, which allowed trains to be 'locked' into the Bilsthorpe branch, while trains continued to run to Rufford and Blidworth.

The colliery closed in April 1997. The last trains ran on 29 April, of which I photographed the final two. The penultimate train was hauled by 58046 *Asfordby Mine* and ran as 7B67 to West Burton power station. The final arrival was 58040 *Cottam Power Station* with 6K98 from Worksop. After loading, and without fanfare, the train departed as 7F98 to Cottam, appropriately enough. Having obtained a photo of the train's arrival at Bilsthorpe, I dashed over to Clipstone forest for the long walk to Bilsthorpe Junction and photographed this final departure from the branch. The colliery was soon demolished, with the headstocks being brought down with explosives on 31 October 1997.

Calverton

The London Midland and Scottish Railway (LMS) and London and North Eastern Railway (LNER) jointly proposed the Mid-Notts Joint Railway from Bestwood Park Junction, on the former Leen Valley Line (near Nottingham), to a junction at Checker House, on the former GCR line between Worksop and Retford. Only the section between Farnsfield and Ollerton was built, but a 7-mile section from Bestwood Park was completed in the 1950s to serve the new Calverton Colliery.

A decision was made to sink a mine shaft in Calverton in 1936, and on 14 June 1937, the first sod was cut by Captain C.B. Lancaster and Sir Hugh Seely. No. 1 shaft was completed at a depth of 576 yards on 22 May 1939. Although the pit top buildings and several houses for the workers were erected, the outbreak of the Second World War put a halt to proceedings. Work recommenced on a second shaft in 1946, being completed in 1952, and the coal preparation plant came into use in 1954. The sidings at the colliery were built by Holloway Bros (contractors), but a rapid-loading bunker with a capacity of 2,000 tons was commissioned in September 1968.

The pit broke the weekly production record of 40,500 tons in 1992. By unfortunate timing, British Coal announced the pit's closure in that same week, but this was later changed to a reduction in workforce.

Another change of plan saw British Coal close the colliery on 19 November 1993. However, this was not quite the end as on 23 May 1994, RJB Mining leased the mine for a ten-year period, with a promise to increase the workforce from 150 to 300. RJB extended their lease to twenty-five years in 1996, but the following year, they suspended all investment in the colliery. A press release issued on 9 April 1999 stated:

> Mining was to cease at Calverton Colliery and the operating lease and licence returned to owners The Coal Authority by current licensee operators RJB Mining. Calverton was closed by British Coal in 1993 and reopened by RJB the following year. Since then the mine has produced over 2.5 million tons of coal. But RJB announced today that deteriorating geological conditions in the limited remaining accessible reserves, leading to higher production costs, have made ongoing operations unviable, both now and in the foreseeable future. Production at Calverton will cease next week.

Production finished at the colliery on 16 April 1999, with the mine closing altogether from 9 July. The closure marked the end of coal mining in the Leen Valley north of Nottingham. Shaft filling and demolition was swift; No. 2 shaft was filled in September and the demolition of the colliery buildings began from 29 October. No. 1 headgear was demolished on 19 January 2000. The rapid-loading bunker went on 6 February, with No. 2 headgear succumbing seven days later.

Calverton attracted many photographers during its final months, both in the colliery area and along the branch, particularly where it paralleled the Robin Hood line at Bestwood Park. I managed several shots in different locations, some of which are featured here.

The first train I photographed at Calverton Colliery was this one on 23 June 1994. Having found the location, it was a mad dash to get in position as 56100 was already under the bunker having arrived as 6J25 from Milford, before it was to set back to the loading pad for loading.

Moving from the field at the bunker end of the colliery, I made my way to the pad loading area where 56100 has now run around its train and is being loaded by mechanical shovel on 23 June 1994.

After loading, 56100 is now seen as it departs Calverton with 7C61 to Milford on 23 June 1994.

No. 60012 *Glyder Fawr* is seen while loading 7A20 Calverton to Ratcliffe power station under the bunker at Calverton on 8 May 1996.

After loading beneath the bunker, Mainline Blue livery 58046 *Asfordby Mine* now runs around its train at Calverton to form 7A11 on the 8.35 a.m. to Ratcliffe power station on 10 May 1999. The sidings to the right of the train would once have been full of 16-ton wagons but are now out of use.

Above: A wide-angle view of the Calverton complex as 58046 *Asfordby Mine* now prepares to depart as 7A11 on the 8.35 a.m. to Ratcliffe power station on 10 May 1999.

Below: On 12 May 1999, 58041 *Ratcliffe Power Station* works 7A11 Calverton to Ratcliffe power station and approaches the end of the Calverton branch at Bestwood Park, the single line in the foreground being the 'Robin Hood' line to Worksop.

On the final day of trains from the colliery, it became a bit of a pilgrimage for other photographers. Here two other photographers are inside the colliery complex as 58046 *Asfordby Mine* is loaded beneath the bunker to form the final train from the colliery on 20 May 1999. This was 7A11 Calverton to Ratcliffe power station.

Dashing from the colliery, I made it to Moor Road crossing at Bestwood Park to catch the train coming along the end of the Calverton branch, and here is 58046 *Asfordby Mine* with 7A11 Calverton to Ratcliffe power station, this being the final train off the branch.

As the train was held at the branch end signal, I had chance to get to Moor Road overbridge to catch 58046 passing Bestwood Park signal box. This area has changed considerably, the box has gone and Nottingham trams now run alongside Robin Hood line passenger trains here.

Clipstone

In 1912, the Bolsover Colliery Company leased 6,000 acres of mining rights from the duke of Portland, and a test bore found the 6-foot-thick top hard seam at a depth of 640 yards. The sinking work was suspended at a depth of 50 feet at the outbreak of the First World War in 1914, but the surface buildings went on to be completed. Work on shaft-sinking recommenced in 1919, and by 1922, two 21-foot-diameter shafts were complete. Mining on the top hard seam began in 1927, but with the seam being worked out by the Second World War, a programme of reconstruction was drawn up just after the war by the NCB, which implemented the scheme upon nationalisation in 1947–48.

By 1953, work had commenced. The steam-winding system was scrapped along with demolition of most of the surface buildings, to be replaced by new heapsteads, headframes, a fan house, and a winder/power house located between the two shafts, with two electrically powered winders.

The new winding system was of the Koepe type and Clipstone was one of the first post-war examples of this system, built with ground-based winders, which required the use of headframes. The ones at Clipstone have pulley wheels or 'sheaves' located one above the other, being designed specifically for the Koepe winding system. The central winder house containing the two electrically-driven Koepe winders was a modern design of brick and glass. The two headframes stood approximately 65 metres high when built, making them the tallest in the UK.

Despite being profitable, the colliery was one of thirty-one mines named for closure by British Coal; it was closed and mothballed in 1993. RJB Mining took over and reopened the mine in 1994, being the first to restart production under licence arrangements before the privatisation of the NCB had been completed.

Clipstone was once dual-served by the LMS and LNER, but latterly, only the former LNER access to the colliery's loaded wagon sidings was used. A bridge on the colliery branch also allowed the LMS access to the loaded wagon sidings, their line being in a cutting. When I started photography at Clipstone, the LMS route had been disused for some time, and the cutting was being infilled with household waste together with its attendant smells. Once infilling was complete, the land was covered in topsoil and landscaped to make a usable field.

One particular day, I visited the site for a photo, but a tractor was busy spraying evil-smelling manure over the field so I did not hang around. A few weeks later, I returned to find a field full of tomato plants, and although the fruits looked nice enough, I will let the reader think about why the plants were there and why I did not pick any. Over the following months, the field hosted sheep that ate the tomato plants, and eventually, there was no sign of either the former railway or the tomatoes.

One train that attracted the photographers' attention was the Clipstone (but sometimes originating from Welbeck) to Walton Old Junction at Warrington, with coal for export to Ireland. This train, which usually consisted of PFA wagons, ran depending on demand. Table 6 shows the timings for the Cawoods Containers services, which being for March 2000 is really just outside of the scope of the book but is a worthwhile inclusion. I managed to photograph the Clipstone service in numerous locations on different occasions.

Table 6: Cawoods Containers Week Commencing 12 March 2000						Su	M	T	W	Th	F	S
6B27	05.39	TTHO	Swansea Burrows	Cardiff Docks	08.30	-	-	C	-	C	-	-
6B32	11.15	TTHO	Cardiff Docks	Swansea Burrow	13.36	-	-	C	-	C	-	-
6P97	05.51	MO	Walton Old Sdgs	Seaforth	08.18	-	S1	-	-	-	-	-
6Z58	11.05	MO	Seaforth	Gascoigne Wood	16.00	-	S1	-	-	-	-	-
6Z89	00.35	THO	Gascoigne Wood	Seaforth	04.58	-	-	-	-	S1	-	-
0P50	05.58	THO	Seaforth	Warrington HS	07.20	-	-	-	-	S1	-	-
0P51	13.09	THO	Warrington HS	Seaforth	14.54	-	-	-	-	S1	-	-
6P51	16.00	THO	Seaforth	Walton Old Sdgs	18.29	-	-	-	-	S1	-	-
6Z53	00.22	SO	Walton Old Sdgs	Clipstone	06.42	-	-	-	-	-	-	S1
6Z86	14.00	SO	Clipstone	Walton Old Sdgs	20.04	-	-	-	-	-	-	S1
		S1 = SET 1 SEAFORTH		C = CANCELLED								

Clipstone resumed production with an anticipated lifespan of six–seven years; it exceeded this by one year, and after a life of just over eighty years, coal-cutting ceased on 17 April 2003. With the final train running on 24 June 2003, the colliery had produced nearly 4 million tons of coal since reopening.

No. 58007 *Drakelow Power Station* is seen while loading 7G37 for Ratcliffe at Clipstone Colliery on 13 June 1994, this being the first departure from the colliery after R. J. Budge took over operations.

Above: After being loaded and travelling into the run-round loop at Rufford Junction, 58019 *Shirebrook Colliery* now departs the loop and heads towards Clipstone Junction with 7G37 Clipstone to West Burton power station on 14 June 1994.

Below: No. 58031 in grey livery with the Mainline 'rolling wheels' decals departs Clipstone Colliery with 7G50 for West Burton on 28 October 1995.

No. 60016 *Langdale Pikes* propels down to Clipstone Colliery with 6Z54 Walton Old Junction to Clipstone to make 6Z82 Clipstone to Walton Old Junction export coal on 28 October 1995. The field in the foreground is the one mentioned in the text.

With the Transrail 'Big T' decals, 60056 *William Beveridge* with 6T65 empties from Thoresby backs down the short branch to Clipstone Colliery on 15 January 1997.

No. 56049 in the former engineers 'Dutch' livery with Transrail brandings is loading 6Z91 Clipstone to Seaforth container terminal at Clipstone on 21 January 1999.

The headgear and winder house were Grade 2-listed in 2000 as an 'early example of the "Koepe" system', stated as being the earliest example left *in situ* in the UK. After closure, the offices and shower blocks were demolished, and in 2003, a referendum in Clipstone was held, and the villagers voted for demolition of the whole site. However, everything except the headstocks, the winder house, and other immediate buildings were demolished, including the baths and coal hoppers. Hopes are for the remaining site and headstocks to be retained and redeveloped into an adventure park featuring a mile-long zip wire.

Gedling

The Digby Colliery Company commenced the sinking of Gedling Colliery in March 1900 and found twenty-seven seams of coal varying from a few inches to 3 feet 9 inches, before the 5-foot 2-inch-thick top hard was reached at a depth of 459 yards in September 1902. In 1937, the Digby Colliery Company, Bestwood Colliery Company, and Babbington Colliery Company merged to become the Bestwood Amalgamated Collieries Ltd. The pit was nationalised in 1947 and become part of the NCB South Nottinghamshire Area from 1967.

Originally, the top hard and main bright seams were worked, but the main bright seam was not worked during the First World War. It was abandoned in 1918 but reopened and was worked from 1933–1940, then again from

1967–1968 before a final attempt to work it began in 1987–88, ending at closure in 1991.

The top hard was worked until 1961 when, since it was uneconomical to mine further, the seam was abandoned. The High Hazels seam was first developed in 1927 and was worked until August 1961 when it too was abandoned.

The last coal was extracted on 7 November 1991. During its life, almost 70 million tons of coal was produced from the three seams, of which 20 per cent was steam coal and the remainder household lump coal.

The colliery was originally served by a spur from the former Great Northern Railway (GNR) Derbyshire and Staffordshire Line, which ran from Netherfield Junction on the GNR Nottingham to Grantham line, via Colwick (and its marshalling yard) and Gedling, to Daybrook and eventually Derby. With the closure of Mapperley Tunnel in 1960, the remaining section of the line served Gedling Colliery from the Netherfield end.

The final train out of the colliery was on 15 November 1991, when 58012 hauled ten loaded HEAs destined for Aldermaston, and the last passenger train to use the branch was the 'Trent-Wreake' rail tour on 13 February 1993, after which the line was mothballed.

The branch reopened when RJB Mining wanted to remove the substantial 400,000-ton stockpile from the site, for forwarding to Rufford stocking site to be blended. On 30 December 1997, 37114 traversed the route to attend a small ceremony, attended by local councillors, Railtrack, and EWS. Substantial work was required to bring the line back up to standard, including completely fencing it in and improving the level crossing over Victoria Road, Netherfield. The first train ran behind 58049 *Littleton Colliery* as 7Z27 on the 11 a.m. Gedling Colliery to Rufford Stocking Site on 11 December 1998.

Initially, one train per week was booked, arriving at 7 a.m. and departing at 10.30 a.m., but this increased to two or more per week. Routing restrictions ensured that trains were limited to twenty-nine wagons due to the gradient on Pinxton Bank, but they usually avoided Pinxton altogether by running via Toton, Barrow Hill, Woodhouse (run-round), Kiveton, Shireoaks, Shirebrook, and Clipstone Junction.

My first visit to locate the loading site was on 22 December 1998, unfortunately coinciding with poor weather. Despite clear conditions when leaving home, Gedling was reached in thick fog. With no point trying to find the loading point, I ventured to Netherfield and Colwick station where the Gedling branch joined the Nottingham to Grantham line. In the fog, I attempted a poor photo of 58049 *Littleton Colliery* passing the station with 7Z27 on the 10.30 a.m. Gedling to Rufford.

The following month, I returned in good weather, found Gedling loading site, and took some decent photos. I returned a few more times to photograph trains both in the loading site and from vantage points along the branch. The final train ran on 3 November 2000, and the Gedling colliery branch was finally lifted in 2012.

This was the first successful attempt at photos at Gedling, and here 58026 is seen loading 7Z27 on the 10.30 a.m. Gedling Colliery to Rufford stocking site on 21 January 1999. The orange-clad trainman is directing operations as the loco draws forward to allow the next few wagons to be loaded by mechanical shovels.

This view of 58026 with 7Z27 on the 10.30 a.m. Gedling Colliery to Rufford stocking site was taken from the A612 Colwick Loop Road overbridge. Unbelievable as it is, the train is passing the site of the massive Colwick depot and yards, the green area being the northern extent of it. Once the single line here was double track, and the train would have just passed Colwick North Junction; however, with the exception of a few sidings at the south end, by the time of this photo, all the yards had gone.

As viewed from Lambley Lane overbridge, 58005 *Ironbridge Power Station* departs from the site of Gedling Colliery with 7Z27 on the 10.30 a.m. departure to Rufford stocking site on 12 February 1999. I missed the loading that day so had to be content with shots along the branch.

Having dashed from Lambley Lane to Netherfield and Colwick station, I was in time to get a shot of *58005 Ironbridge Power Station* as came off the branch at Netherfield Junction with 7Z27 Gedling to Rufford Stock. The sign reads 'Commencement of Staff Section'.

Turning around from the previous photo, we now see the driver of 7Z27 Gedling to Rufford Stock has just handed the token pouch for the branch to the signalman at Netherfield Junction and is now putting on power to head towards Nottingham.

Returning to the site of the colliery again on 18 May 1999, I was to find 66086 at the head of a train of MEA wagons as it was being loaded to make 6Z61 to Oxcroft Opencast disposal point. This train would be unloaded at Oxcroft and the coal blended with the other coal stocks. The two wagons on the right were cripples awaiting movement away for repairs.

Once the train had been photographed at Gedling, I made my way over to Netherfield to await the train, and here, 66086 is seen waiting for the trainman to open the gates of Victoria Road level crossing, which disappeared when the branch was lifted in 2012, and there is very little to see here now.

Harworth

The Northern Union Mining Company started sinking the shafts for Harworth Colliery (in North Nottinghamshire) in 1913, utilising German men and equipment. Unfortunately, with the outbreak of the First World War, work stopped when the German workers were interned and the company's assets impounded by the government.

In 1917, the pit was bought by Messrs. Barber, Walker and Co., and the shaft-sinking initially recommenced in 1919. The first real sinking did not recommence until 1921. On 29 October 1923, the Barnsley seam was reached by No. 1 shaft at 2,782 feet, followed by No. 2 shaft on 15 November 1923.

The colliery's first rail connection was made from the East Coast Main Line at Scrooby in 1924, but in 1928, a new connection was made from the South Yorkshire Joint Railway between Maltby and Tickhill. The triangular layout was called Firbeck Junction as it also permitted access to the new Firbeck Colliery in Costhorpe between Worksop and Langold.

Harworth was modernised with new concrete headgears in the 1950s, but they were replaced with new headgears in 1989 (No. 1 Shaft) and 1994 (No. 2 shaft). The pit reached the 1 million-tons-per-year figure in 1993.

The first threat of closure came in November 2002 when owners UK Coal issued a warning—unless yearly losses of £8 million could be reversed, the colliery would have to cease operating. In 2005, investment of £50 million to access a new seam was required, which would have produced up to twenty-five years' worth of coal, but it was not to be, and the pit was placed on review, eventually ceasing operation altogether. There were plans to reopen the colliery, and indeed, work started underground to make good the infrastructure in order to access the remaining millions of tons of unmined coal. However, in the end, it came to nothing, and in April 2016, the colliery was demolished to make way for housing.

I photographed many trains heading to and from Harworth around Maltby and the South Yorkshire Joint Railway, but my first photo at the colliery was not taken until 1994, when 58026 was seen loading 7G38 to West Burton on 6 October. I returned several times afterwards to take photos from a road bridge and from wasteland alongside the loading line. On 4 September 2006, Freightliner's 66507 became the final loco to work the colliery branch with 4G05 on the 10 a.m. from Cottam, which formed 6F29 on the 1.48 p.m. back to Cottam. The Harworth colliery branch has not been used since, has been physically disconnected from the South Yorkshire Joint Railway and all trackwork lifted.

After arriving with an empty set of wagons from Worksop, 58041 *Ratcliffe Power Station* has loaded its train and is now running round at Harworth Colliery to depart as 6F53 for Cottam power station on 8 February 1994. The three-lever ground frame on the right is to control access to the former Harworth glass bulbs branch, which can be seen diverging off right. No. 1 lever was the release that could only be pulled with the permission of Maltby Colliery box, No. 2 the points, and No. 3 the signal; this had not been used for some years though.

Right: Something a bit different on 2 October 1997—here, 58032 is seen passing the run-round loop on the approach to Harworth Colliery working as 6W01 Worksop to Harworth. Although it looks like a light loco, there was actually a wagon behind, this being taken to the colliery to perform weights and measure testing with a series of large weights the wagon was conveying.

Below: After delivering the weights to the waiting staff at the bunker, the weights were removed from the wagon by a road crane and placed on the weighbridge for testing to begin. Meanwhile, the loco pushed the wagon back into the run-round loop to run round. Here, 58032 is seen waiting to run round.

Testing complete and after running round, the weights are replaced back into the wagon ready to be returned to Worksop.

An unusual event occurred on 17 July 1997 when 37375 and 37703 were turned out to work a Toton to Harworth Colliery train, and here they are seen after loading and running around at Harworth to form 7G41 Harworth to Toton, with coal for Ratcliffe power station.

Dashing from Harworth, the next location to get a photo was Firbeck Cutting on the South Yorkshire Joint Railway. Here, 37375 and 37703 pass with 7G41 Harworth to Toton.

Manton

In 1897, the Wigan Coal and Iron Co. began sinking a new colliery at Manton, just south-east of Worksop, on land owned by Henry Pelham-Clinton (the 7th duke of Newcastle), to work the top hard or Barnsley seam. This seam was found at a depth of 718 yards. Coal mining began in June 1905 and continued until 1964. The Parkgate seam was worked between 1962 and 1994, and in 1991, production from the Flockton seam began.

At nationalisation of the collieries, Manton (although in Nottinghamshire) became part of the South Yorkshire area. In 1979, over 1 million tons of coal was mined, most being sent straight to Cottam power station. The miners' strike of 1984–85 hit the colliery and the miners who worked there hard, including my father who worked there. After the strike, Manton was still a profitable pit, and it celebrated a landmark of 1 million tons in a year.

The rail side converted to MGR operations in the late 1980s, dispensing with the need for internal shunting locos. As such, the last two in operation—ex-British Rail Class 04 0-6-0 D2229 (NCB No. 5) and Hudswell Clarke 0-6-0 No. D1159—were side-lined. Both have since been preserved: D2229 is part of the Heritage Shunters Trust fleet at Rowsley, on Peak Rail, while the Hudswell Clarke loco was last heard of at the Midland Railway Butterley.

The colliery still produced large amounts of coal with a good market of Cottam power station, just before it was forced to close in 1994. Manton was the twenty-ninth British colliery to close in the space of a year, as part of the pit closure programme led by Prime Minister Margaret Thatcher, who claimed UK coal production was outweighing demand as huge stockpiles grew. The February 1994 issue of *Coal News* reported that Manton would close in the middle of that month, and indeed, it did on 11 February. The bulldozers soon moved in, and the pithead buildings were removed. The shafts were infilled with large amounts of limestone and concrete, and the headstocks were demolished with explosives on 6 December 1994. Today, a B&Q distribution warehouse occupies the site.

Manton Colliery was where my father worked, and although it was on our doorstep, I took it for granted until it was almost due for closure, hence I have very few photos of the colliery. It was just a short walk from my parents' house to the colliery spoil heap, which allowed a view of the loading area. From here, the already-mentioned out-of-use shunting locos could be seen, along with the remaining single track of the headshunt for the pad unloading line.

Following demolition, the stockpiled coal needed shifting, and in 1995, operations began removing it to Cottam. However, in September 1995, the coal was rejected as being too wet, causing it to stick to the wagons, and operations ceased. After the coal was turned to reduce its water content, a second attempt was made. On 27 September 1996, 58033 took out 7F86 on the 10.41 a.m. Manton to Cottam. The operation was very short-lived, and barely a fortnight later on 4 October 1996, the final train from Manton to Cottam power station ran behind 58036.

Since then, nothing has used the branch, and after the construction of the B&Q warehouse, the line has been fenced off.

No. 58046 *Thoresby Colliery* is dwarfed by the pithead buildings at Manton Colliery as it loads 7F55 for Cottam power station on 30 May 1993. MGR-style trains at Manton were pad-loaded, the pad being to the left of the conveyors passing over the loco. The former loading screens were in the building to the right of the loco, the concrete piles it stands on each showing where the tracks went into the building, and coal of varying sizes was loaded into conventional wagons in days gone.

After loading, 58046 now runs round its train and will couple to the other end. Once ready to depart from the colliery, it will make its way towards the main line connection, which is in the distance next to the red brick water tower.

Above: No. 58046 now makes its way from the colliery to Manton Wood Junction, where it will gain the main line after a shunt move. It will then head off to Cottam power station.

Below: Here is 56007 is loading 7F49 for Cottam power station on 9 February 1994, the colliery closed two days later on 11 February 1994.

Out of use at Manton Colliery were Class 04 D2229 along with Hudswell Clarke Works No. D1159 of 1959. Both were later preserved the Hudswell Clarke last seen on the Midland Railway-Butterley while the Class 04 is at Peak Rail.

Once the colliery had closed and demolition had been completed, the remaining coal stocks were removed. The first Class 58 in EW&S red was 58033, and here it is setting back along the Manton Colliery branch as 6K86 from Worksop to Manton for loading on 27 September 1996.

No. 58033 is now having its train loaded at the loading pad while the TP waits in his yellow van on 27 September 1996. This train would be the first train out of the colliery sidings since September 1995 and would go forward as 7F86 on the 10.41 a.m. Manton to Cottam.

Mainline blue-liveried 58036 climbs up the colliery branch towards the main line connection with 7F86 Fridays only 10.41 a.m. Manton to Cottam on 4 October 1996, this being the final train from Manton.

Ollerton

November 1923 saw the commencement of shaft-sinking for Ollerton Colliery by Francoise Cementation Co. Ltd. The company was established in 1910 by Albert Francois, a Belgian who had been striving to improve grouting associated with shaft-sinking for coal mining, as the Francois Cementation Company based at Doncaster. They had a patent process of freezing the water as they proceeded with digging operations. The shafts were completed by the Butterley Company, who reached coal on 4 August 1925, with production commencing in August 1926 from a 'tub and stall' and rope-haulage system. The total cost of establishing the colliery, including new housing for the workers, was about £1,500,000.

The first train of coal left the colliery on 1 September 1926 hauled by LNER N6 0-6-2T 6413, driven by Edward Hutchinson and fired by Charles Fox, the guard being Joseph Pickering, all from Tuxford depot. The train consisted of just two wagons destined for Booth and Warren of St Ives in Huntingdonshire. Wagon BG 1612 carried 7-ton 10-cwt NETT of hand-picked brights, while LNWR No. 75371 contained 8-ton 12-cwt NETT of hand-picked hards.

Ollerton was nationalised on 1 January 1947, forming part of the East Midlands division of the NCB. The NCB set production targets for each colliery—in Ollerton's case, 17,500 tons of saleable coal per week (910,000 tons per year). When the target was met, the NCB flag was raised on No. 1 headstock. During the early 1950s, to handle the ever-increasing production, a diesel-hauled high-capacity mine car system, state-of-the-art underground rail track and signalling unit, high-capacity mine car loading points, and fully mechanised coal handling machinery were installed underground.

On the surface, high-capacity conveyors, mine car unloading machinery, and an updated screening plant were also incorporated into the new scheme, which came into use at Easter in 1953. These new units had many benefits over the old, such that they could handle greater tonnage, required less maintenance, and, importantly, reduced the manpower needed.

By the afternoon of 7 December 1968, a major milestone for the colliery had been reached—1 million tons had been raised in one year. The top hard seam finally produced its last coal in December 1978. During its life of fifty-two years, it had produced over 37 million tons from 100 faces. Access to the Parkgate seam, 180 yards below the top hard, was started in 1974, coming on stream in February 1977.

By 1986, there were 1,240 employed at the colliery (plus seven canaries), and production was running at 4,500 tons per day. Four-fifths of the coal produced went to Trent Valley power stations by rail, while the remainder went to industrial users, some of them abroad. Towards the end of the colliery's life, the main customers were High Marnham and Cottam power stations, accounting for 85 per cent of saleable output, the rest being for the domestic market in Northern Ireland and home markets. Production from the Parkgate seam at Ollerton Colliery ceased when the last skip of coal was wound, and the colliery closed at the beginning of 1994.

It was possible to photograph trains at this colliery from a disused rail overbridge that once served the Rexco smokeless coal plant at Ollerton. However, there were other spots to obtain images, such as another long-closed railway bridge abutment to the east of the colliery. The highlight of my photography at Ollerton was when I obtained a cab ride through the bunker, thanks to a generous driver that I knew.

The colliery closed on 12 February 1994. On 25 February 1994, the final train arrived from Worksop as 6F45 with 58007 *Drakelow Power Station* at the helm, to form 7F45 on the 1.06 p.m. service to Cottam. I photographed the train from the disused bridge abutments as it arrived at the colliery sidings.

The colliery was demolished shortly after closure, and the headstocks were felled on 20 December 1994. However, around 200,000 tons of stockpiled, mainly power station coal remained unsold. This was moved to a temporary loading pad adjacent to the former bunker line in the sidings area, prior to being loaded into awaiting trains. The first such arrival was 6C28 from Toton behind 58004 on 6 June 1995, which departed as 7A29 to Ratcliffe power station. I photographed the train while being loaded, and I returned to Ollerton several times before trains stopped running.

Having blagged a ride on the loco, this is the view of the loading bunker at Ollerton from the seat of 58041 *Ratcliffe Power Station* on 12 February 1994.

As viewed from Ollerton Colliery signal box, 58041 *Ratcliffe Power Station* passes Ollerton Colliery with 6F45 from Worksop on 12 February 1994. It will enter the reception sidings where it will run round and then pull through the bunker to form 7F45 for Cottam power station.

The train has now passed through the bunker, and 58041 is now ready to set back and begin loading 7F45 for Cottam power station at Ollerton on 12 February 1994.

Staying at Ollerton for a few hours meant I could then photograph the second arrival on 12 February 1994, this being 58026, and here it is standing on the bunker line at Ollerton with the signal box on right, ready to load 7A30 for Ratcliffe power station.

No. 58026 has now pulled through the bunker and is setting back for loading 7A30 for Ratcliffe power station.

A few days later and after a fall of snow, another visit to Ollerton was made. Here as viewed from the long-closed Mid-Notts Joint Line bridge abutment, 58007 is dropping into the reception sidings with 6F45 from Worksop, on 25 February 1994.

After the closure of the colliery, the stockpiled coal had to be removed and here with a cab full of staff and surrounded by dignitaries, 58004 is loaded with coal from the closed and demolished Ollerton Colliery site. This would form 6C28 for Drakelow power station and be the first train from the stockpile on 6 June 1995.

A second view of 58004 as it is loaded with coal from the stockpile to form 6C28 for Drakelow power station on 6 June 1995. The lines in the foreground are two now disused sidings.

This is the view of the closed and demolished Ollerton Colliery site from the long-closed Mid-Notts Joint Railway bridge abutment, as 58004 is loaded with stockpiled coal on 6 June 1995. It will form 6C28 for Drakelow power station.

Rufford Colliery and Rufford Stock Site

In 1911, the Bolsover Colliery Company Ltd leased land from Lord Savile and sank two shafts to access the top hard seam—the 21-foot-diameter No. 1 and the 18-foot No. 2. The colliery was so called because the seams were under a portion of the Rufford Abbey estate. The branch from Rufford Colliery opened on 8 July 1918, and the colliery was soon turning out in excess of 4,400 tons per day.

As the development of the colliery continued down to the low main seam, between August 1953 and February 1955, No. 2 shaft was deepened to 857 yards, and between July 1952 and December 1956, a third shaft was sunk to a depth of 877 yards; skip winding was also installed from the low main seam. New electric winders were installed at all three shafts, tower-mounted friction winders on Nos 2 and 3 shafts, and a ground-mounted drum winder on No. 1. Further new buildings were constructed, including a new coal preparation plant, along with the relaying of the empty sidings and full sidings.

The top hard seam was last worked on 17 September 1969, and there was a threat of closure, but by 1972, the colliery was said to be 'the largest in the North Notts Coalfield employing over 1,500 men, but was still suffering with a shortage of staff'. Rufford was the only colliery in the area with three operational shafts, and with vast reserves of coal, it was said that 'the threat of closure had been completely removed'. Also as the pit was going into a new seam, it 'had a better future and was expected to work well into the next century'.

The low main seam ceased production on 1 May 1974. In 1976, skip winding facilities were installed in No. 1 shaft in conjunction with a 400-ton capacity bunker and conveyor system in the High Hazels seam. In week ending 11 November 1990, the colliery produced a record 41,100 tons and was regarded as 'having turned a corner' with two new faces being brought on stream, but others were required to keep the pit on budget. In the mid-1970s, 2,000 tons of coal left the colliery each day from the ex-GCR side, destined for some domestic users and Cottam and West power stations, whereas 750 tons left via the former MR connections.

Despite the above positivity, the colliery was denied a long future as it closed on 26 November 1993. Once again, the stockpile needed removing. On 18 March 1994, I went to the colliery and photographed 58034 *Bassetlaw* departing with 7R50 for Grimethorpe Coalite. By 1995, the colliery had been demolished, and my next visit was on 6 February 1995 to photograph 58033 departing the former colliery area with 7G22 for Rugeley power station. The colliery area was by then known as Rufford Pad, as this was where the blended coal from the adjacent Rufford stocking site was sent out.

I made several visits to Rufford stocking site, entailing a long walk through Clipstone forest to reach a footpath that crossed the site, via two trainman-operated level crossings entitled Elmsley and Inkersall. I obtained some shots of a train discharging its load at the bunker, which was set into the former Blidworth branch, and at some of the crossings.

No. 58034 *Bassetlaw* crosses Elmsley level crossing as it leaves Rufford Colliery with 7R50 to Grimethorpe Coalite on 18 March 1994. The colliery was closed at the time, and the coal stocks were in the process of removal, the trains being sent out via the former LMS side of the colliery towards the connection with the former LNER side of the colliery.

Arriving at the former LNER side of the Rufford complex and surrounded by mounds of coal waiting to be blended, 58030 crosses Inkersall level crossing at Rufford stock site with 7G61 from Daw Mill on 6 February 1995. Instead of lowering the road barriers, the travelling train preparer has used his van to block the crossing.

Having run around its train, 58030 is seen on the discharge line at Rufford Stock Site on 6 February 1995, this was the former Blidworth Colliery branch, which by this time was truncated just beyond the end of the train.

Also taken on 6 February 1995 was this image on the former LMS side of the complex again, where by now the colliery had mostly been demolished. Here 58033 is departing the former colliery area, which was then known as Rufford Pad as that was where blended coal was loaded by mechanical shovel into trains. This train was 7G22 destined for Rugeley power station.

Thoresby

The Bolsover Colliery Company began construction of their last Nottinghamshire colliery in 1925. Although close to Edwinstowe, in the heart of Sherwood Forest, it was named Thoresby Colliery after the nearby Thoresby Hall. Coal was reached at 753 yards on 5 May 1928, with production beginning the same year. It was the first pit in the country to be built with electric winding; it was thus devoid of a boiler house and associated chimney.

The colliery was served by a 0.75-mile curving branch line, diverging from the former LD&ECR Langwith Junction to Lincoln line at 17.25 miles (see the author's *Lancashire, Derbyshire, and East Coast Railway Volume 2* from Fonthill Media for more details of this line). The branch prescribed a 180-degree curve from west to east to reach the colliery sidings. Three further sidings and a run-round loop were provided on the main line at Thoresby Colliery Junction, the signal box of which was provided with a thirty-lever frame, of which twenty-five were working and five spare.

In 1951, Thoresby became the first nationalised pit to exceed an output of 1 million tons in one year. The shafts were deepened by 358 feet in the 1950s, the mine being one of the most productive and profitable in Europe for many years. Coal seams worked by or available to the pit included the Parkgate (from 1994 following closure of Ollerton Colliery), the Deep Soft, and the High Hazels, but work was abandoned within the latter in 1983. In 1983, Thoresby went on to produce 2 million tons in forty-three working weeks.

The rail operations changed with the advent of MGR working, and a new rapid-loading bunker was commissioned on 5 August 1978, which also saw the end of the use of the screens and sidings.

After privatisation in 1994, the mine was taken over by RJB Mining, which later became UK Coal. The primary reserves at Thoresby lay within the Parkgate seam and numbered some 15.6 million tons at a depth of 900 yards. Another 8.7 million tons of resources lay to the north of the colliery within the deep soft seam, at a depth of around 929 yards. To the south-west, the High Hazels seam offered another 8.1 million tons of resources in a good-quality seam at a depth of around 550 yards.

In 1990, Thoresby had an output of 2.3 million tons and was sending out an average of eight trains per day to High Marnham, West Burton, and Cottam power stations. By 1993, the colliery was sending an average of 11,500 tons per week to Cottam and 18,000 tons to West Burton, with High Marnham taking in very little by rail.

My first visit to Thoresby was on 17 June 1993, when I made my way to the signal box to chat with Roy Hawke, a well-known character who worked there at the time. Although I made a few more visits in the 1990s, more visits were actually made in the new millennium.

Once one of England's most productive mines, producing 100,000 tons of coal per week, it was announced in April 2014 that the pit would close. Mining ceased at Thoresby Colliery on Friday, 10 July 2015, the colliery's 600 employees having been reduced to 360 by the time of closure. The final train left the colliery on Thursday, 17 September 2015, when Freightliner's 66617 took 6B56 on the 4 p.m. to Cottam power station.

After photographing a train at Goldthorpe Colliery and several around Ferrybridge and Knottingley on 17 June 1993, I headed south to make my first visit to Thoresby Colliery box. Here I took this shot of 58007 about to depart the sidings with 7G54 Thoresby to West Burton.

It was to be a full year before I returned to Thoresby to get this image of a rather smoky 58017 leaving Thoresby with 7G61 taking coal to Rufford stock site for blending on 14 June 1994.

As viewed from the steps of Thoresby Colliery signal box, and with the aid of a 200-mm zoom lens and 2× converter (giving 400 mm), 58027 is seen loading 7G62 for West Burton in Thoresby Colliery on 14 June 1994.

On a bright and sunny 28 October 1995, 58026 arrives at Thoresby with 6C13 from Toton to make 7A05 for Ratcliffe power station.

Moving on another year, 58049 *Littleton Colliery* (recently repainted into EWS livery) departs from Thoresby Colliery sidings, forming 6T21 Thoresby to Bilsthorpe Colliery for loading on 13 October 1996.

The final shot of the 1990s sees 58018 *High Marnham Power Station* with 7B68 Thoresby to West Burton as it sets of from Thoresby Colliery sidings, the wagons being canopy-fitted HDAs. This was on 15 January 1997.

4

Derbyshire Area Collieries

From Nottinghamshire, the next area to examine is the Derbyshire collieries. When the coal industry was nationalised in 1947, there were sixty-eight collieries in Derbyshire; now there are none. The last five pits to close were Renishaw Park (1989), Creswell (1991), Bolsover, Markham, and Shirebrook (all 1993), as such all of the ones I photographed were disposal points for opencast coal.

Denby Opencast Disposal Point

Commencing from a connection to the Midland Main Line at Little Eaton Junction, at milepost 131 close to Derby, the Denby branch was renowned for its hand-operated level crossings along the route.

The Midland Railway (Ripley Branches) Act was passed on 22 July 1848, and by August, a spur from the main line reached Little Eaton, the line opening for freight as far as Ripley in September 1855. A single line with passing loops and sidings for the adjacent collieries and quarries, the stations along the line opened in September 1856. The line north of Ripley to the connection with the Butterley and Swanwick line was closed to passengers in 1926 (the remaining stations closed on 1 June 1930).

Workings along this section of line had ceased by 1934, with the line being severed north of Ripley in 1938. The section north of Marehay Crossing to Ripley was closed in 1963, and the whole branch from Little Eaton Crossing to Denby North became operated as one engine in steam from 2 March 1969.

Following closure of the signal boxes, the gates along the branch were operated by the remaining crossing keeper at Little Eaton station, who assisted the train's secondman and guard, until the latter two roles were done away with nationally as part of the conversion to one-man operation in the late 1980s. Thereafter, brake vans were attached at each end of the train, and trainmen would accompany each train, operating the crossing gates as it progressed. After this method ceased in 1994, a travelling train preparer (TTP) would travel by road to each crossing and operate the gates as required.

The rapid-loading bunker was commissioned in 1991, and the last trains ran in April 1999. No. 58035 hauled what was ostensibly the last train on 16 April, departing as 7C47 on the 8.35 a.m. to Drakelow 'C', after which the single line staff was removed from Little Eaton. As it happened, another train ran on Monday, 19 April 1999, hauled by 66008 as 6T47 Toton to Denby. The driver was in for a surprise, however, as he was stopped outside Derby PSB and handed the staff for the branch. There was insufficient coal for a full train, so the half-loaded train departed as 7C47 for Drakelow 'C'. The final move along the branch was a weed-killing train in 2000, following which the line turned into a linear forest until track reclamation took place, with the branch being completely lifted by Friday, 9 March 2012. The opencast sites have also since been restored.

The sedate operation of the branch permitted numerous photos to be taken of each train from various points. Fortunately, the B6179 paralleled the line for most of its length, so it was easy to obtain a photo of the train at each level crossing along the route as the travelling train preparer opened and closed them. I had seen many photographs of trains along the route, but it was not until January 1999 that I made the journey down to Denby to photograph a train. By this time, all trains were Class 58-hauled, but I made several visits to the line during the short period before trains ceased—oh for a time machine.

The first jaunt to Denby was undertaken on 15 February 1999 very late in the day as far as operations were concerned there. Not knowing where to go for photos, I found my way to the bunker area where I arrived just as 58007 *Drakelow Power Station* arrived with 6T50 from Toton to make 7C50 the 2.15 p.m. Denby to Drakelow power station.

We are now at the other end of the bunker and this is the view of 58007 *Drakelow Power Station* from Park Hall Road, which crossed the line here. Still loading 7C50 on the 2.15 p.m. Denby to Drakelow power station, the loco will continue towards the camera as loading continues.

After loading, the train would be pushed back into the run-round loop, and here, 58007 is in the process of running around the train. This is the view from close to a level crossing over Rawson Green.

Now viewed from the level crossing, 58007 is attaching to the rear of its train to go forward as 7C50 on the 2.15 p.m. Denby to Drakelow power station.

Making another visit to the branch on 28 January 1999, we see 58007 once again, this time departing from Denby and crossing the road at Holbrook level crossing with 7C50 on the 2.15 p.m. Denby to Drakelow power station.

A mad dash from the previous shot allowed me to get to the junction with the main Chesterfield to Derby line at Little Eaton Junction at milepost 131, to see 58007 *Drakelow Power Station* as it joins the main line with 7C50 Denby to Drakelow on 28 January 1999.

Some views along the Denby branch begins with 58038 as it passes Little Eaton crossing with 7C47 on the 8.35 a.m. Denby to Drakelow on 24 February 1999.

A view of Coxbench station as the travelling train preparer waits for 58014 as it approaches with 6T47 Toton to Denby on 24 March 1999.

Mainline grey-liveried 58010 trundles along the Denby branch on 15 March 1999 while working 7C47 the 8.25 a.m. for Drakelow power station.

Racing to another location, we now see 58010 as it approaches Holbrook crossing with the 8.25 a.m. departure of 7C47 from Denby for Drakelow on 15 March 1999.

This was the end of the branch, the former Denby station, with the station house on the left. The station opened on 1 September 1856 as Smithy Houses being renamed 'Denbey' from 1 November 1856 and 'Denby' from 1 February 1878. Although it closed to passenger services on 1 June 1930, one of the platforms is still visible in the photo. Here we see 58010 approaching the end of the line while loading 7C47 to Drakelow on 15 March 1999.

Doe Hill Opencast Disposal Point

Doe Hill opencast site was situated alongside the Erewash Valley line and was operated by H. J. Banks. The site had a connection from the bidirectional Down and Up goods line via a ground frame, this being installed when Trent PSB took over the area and Doe Hill signal box was closed. Originally, this gave access to the Doe Hill oil distribution depot. Installed in Doe Hill station goods yard, it had two sidings for tank wagon loading. Originally, the oil siding was served daily, but in later years, trains were down to once a week, and by 1991, they ran as required.

With the decision to opencast the area, the oil siding connection was re-used for a new single-track pad-loading area. Built at right angles to the main line, this became the disposal point for the gleaned coal. As access to the terminal was only available from the south, and with no run-round facilities within the site, trains from the Toton direction had to travel past the location before the loco was detached. The light engine continued north to Clay Cross Junction, crossed over, and returned south to Blackwell Junction before re-coupling to the opposite end of the train. The loco would then propel the train into the site.

In late 1995, Mainline Freight won the contract to move coal from the site, and the first such train ran on 10 October hauled by 58009. This was the only train I would get to photograph at Doe Hill, and I recall standing on the overbridge at Stonebroom Lane, waiting for it to appear from the north after the train loco had ran around. It came around the curve, stopped, and then set back into the loading area. It departed the site as 6R71 on the 2.45 p.m. to Ratcliffe power station.

Doe Hill opencast site was projected to last for five years and dispatch three trains a week to Ratcliffe, but it would also send trains to Drax at the rate of one per day, which ran as 7E62.

Once Doe Hill opencast site was exhausted on one side of the Erewash Valley line, it was closed down but a new one to the west of the line was opened, being connected to the main site by an underbridge. This site was called Stonebroom and was worked between 20 November 2000 and 23 March 2002, and some 269,084 tons of coal recovered. Although trains continued to run in that time, I never went back until well after operations had been completed.

Renishaw Park Opencast Disposal Point

A new opencast loading site opened alongside the former Midland Railway 'Old Road' between Beighton Junction and Barrow Hill in 1998. Operated by the Banks Group Mining Division, the loading site was close to the site of Renishaw Park Colliery, which had closed in 1989.

Coal won from the opencast site was transported by an internal haul road, across the B6053 Slayley Lane to a grading and storage area adjacent to the railway. Here, a pad loading site was provided alongside a new siding accessed via a re-laid connection to the Down Barrow Hill line. The site was laid with a good covering of red shale

No. 58009 arrives at Doe Hill on 10 October 1995 with first train to enter the site, it will continue past the camera and then set back into the siding, the connection being opposite the orange-clad figure.

Above: Almost there—the loco continues to set back into the site, while on the right, the stockpiled coal can be seen adjacent to the loading pad.

Below: The driver continues looking back as the train reverses into the siding at Doe Hill. The person on the track was another photographer, his image being published in *Rail* magazine that month.

obtained from the long-closed Hartington Colliery spoil heap, around half a mile to the south.

To access the pad-loading siding, trains left the Down line and ran into a shunt neck. From there, they reversed into the pad line where mechanical shovels loaded the train. Loaded trains set back through a crossover on to the Up line, then ran to Barrow Hill to run around. From there, trains re-traced their steps past the site, destined for Eggborough power station.

Trains commenced in the first week of October 1998 and operated daily, arriving at 9.53 a.m. and departing at 11.53 a.m., and ran to Eggborough. I managed to gain access to the site twice thanks to an obliging site manager, to whom I send belated thanks.

The opencast mine was a short-lived operation, open for just two years as the license to extend the site was refused. Even so, 300,000 tons of coal was extracted before the site was returned to agricultural use. Today, you would not know there had ever been an opencast site there.

On my first visit, not long after Renishaw Opencast disposal point site had opened to rail traffic, on 8 October 1998, I found Loadhaul livery 56106 in the sidings loading 7C03 for Eggborough.

Opposite above: While photographing 56106, passing on the main line is 58032 *Thoresby Colliery* working an empty set from Worksop to Oxcroft Opencast disposal point.

Opposite middle: The second and only other visit was this one on 23 October 1998 in which 58018 *High Marnham Power Station* can be seen as it loads 7C07 for Eggborough power station. The 'Old Road' between Barrow Hill and Beighton Junction is on the right.

Opposite below: A second view of 58018 *High Marnham Power Station* as it loads 7C07 for Eggborough power station on 23 October 1998.

Seymour Stocking Site

In September 1996, a project to clear up the Seymour sidings area was started, and while doing so, a large amount of buried, low-quality coal was discovered. This was reclaimed and taken to the long-closed Seymour Colliery site, where a temporary train-loading pad was created alongside the former Seymour Colliery branch.

The Seymour area had developed over the years, and by the early parts of the twentieth century, it had become an extremely busy area, with numerous sidings for sorting the coal from the area's collieries. Seymour Colliery was a product of the Staveley Company and had been named after one of its directors. Shaft-sinking commenced in 1855, with production starting from the top hard seam in 1858. However, the mine was closed in July 1918, and the site and its workers cottages were demolished in 1932.

The first train to arrive for loading at the newly-opened reclaimed coal site, and indeed, the first to enter the former colliery branch siding in over seven years was hauled by 58007 *Drakelow Power Station* as 6K70 Worksop to Seymour on 24 September 1996. After loading, it departed as 7B70 to West Burton.

A mixture of classes 56 and 58 were used to move the stockpile, and I managed several visits to the area for photography, in all weathers. What was supposed to be the final train from the site was hauled away by 56089 as 7H12 Seymour to Drax power station, leaving at 3.02 p.m. on 28 January 1997, but as the captions to the images tell, that was not to be the case.

Opposite above: Sections of the down pages of the train register book (TRB) from Seymour Junction. Although the top of the page is dated Friday, 13 December 1996, only parts are shown from Monday 16 December and Tuesday 17 December. The signalmen have annotated the advance section of the page with the destination of the trains—Bolsover, Oxcroft, and Stock, which is Seymour stock site.

Opposite below: The corresponding sections of the up pages of the TRB from the same dates as the down pages, which shows the origins of the trains—again, Bolsover, Oxcroft, and Stock.

Derbyshire Area Collieries

B.R. 24847

DOWN

Signal Box: SEYMOUR JN.
FRI day, 13. day of DEC. 19 96.

Description of Train	REAR SECTION – Is Line Clear – Received but not accepted	Accepted under Regulation 3. clause 3.5 or Permissive (2-4-2)	Regulation 3. clause 3.4	Train approaching Signal received	Train entering Section	Train out of Section sent	Train description received	Train arrived	Train departed or passed	Line	ADVANCE SECTION – Is Line Clear – Offered but not accepted	Accepted Regulation 3. clause 3.5 or Permissive (2-4-2)	Regulation 3. clause 3.4	Train approaching Signal sent	Train entering Section sent	Train out of Section received	Train description sent	Remarks
					MONDAY 16th DECEMBER													
	Box open to SPB at 0520 S. Wildsmith on duty																	
7Y41					0521	0530	0533										Bolsover	
6E10	Waiting T.A.				0526	0536	0601										Oxcroft	
0T50						0903	0910										Oxcroft	
	Clock correct at 0922																	
6R83						1129	1140										Stock	
6R84					1125	1135											Stock	
6Z62					1630	1640	1910										Oxc	TP
0Y42						1935	.45										Bols	
				TUESDAY 17th DECEMBER														
	Box open to SPB at 0525 S. Wildsmith on duty																	
7Y41					0632	0640	0650										Bolsover	
6E10						0746	0753										Oxcroft	
0Z99					0750	0754	0823										Oxcroft	
6R83						1138	1149										Stock	
	S. Wildsmith off duty 1355.																	

Signal Box: SEYMOUR JN.
FRI day, 13. day of DEC. 19 96.

B.R. 24847

UP

Description of Train	REAR SECTION – Is Line Clear – Received but not accepted	Accepted Regulation 3. clause 3.5 or Permissive (2-4-2)	Regulation 3. clause 3.4	Train approaching Signal received	Train entering Section	Train out of Section sent	Train description received	Train arrived	Train departed or passed	Line	ADVANCE SECTION – Is Line Clear – Offered but not accepted	Accepted Regulation 3. clause 3.5 or Permissive (2-4-2)	Regulation 3. clause 3.4	Train approaching Signal sent	Train entering Section sent	Train out of Section received	Train description sent	Remarks
					MONDAY 16th DECEMBER													
0D02	Ex Bolsover							0600									0558	
0E10	Ex Oxcroft							0625									0624	
4H11	Ex Oxcroft							1005									1003	
	16 Exchanged SPB 1020 Equipment Tested OK																	
	S. Wildsmith off duty 1350																	
	D. Talbot on 1350																	
4H14	Stock.							1400									1400	
4H18	Stock.							1455									1455	
6Y42	Bols.							1850									1850	
6Z64	Oxc.							1900									.55	
	Box closed D. Talbot off 1905																	
					TUESDAY 17th DECEMBER													
0D02	Ex Bolsover							0716									0715	
0E10	Ex Oxcroft							0816									0816	
	16 Exchanged SPB 10.00 Equipment Tested OK																	
4H11	Ex Oxcroft							1013									1005	
	D. Talbot on 1355																	

No. 58007 *Drakelow Power Station* passes Seymour Junction box on 24 September 1996, with 6K70 from Worksop for loading at Seymour stock site.

Above: After loading, 58007 *Drakelow Power Station* departs from Seymour stock site with 7B70 for West Burton power station. This was the first train in over seven years to use the stock site siding.

Below: When EWS purchased the freight companies, there was some delay before they settled on a livery. As such, any locos that were undergoing repaints were turned out in a grey undercoat, and here, 56068 is seen arriving at Seymour stock site as it propels down to the loading pad on 4 October 1996.

No. 56068 is now adjacent to the pad loading area and when loaded will form 7H11 Seymour to Drax power station. Notice the large amount of coal waiting to be loaded.

Loading continues in all weathers, and here on a very cold and misty 25 January 1997, Transrail livery 56038 *Western Mail* is loading 7H18 Seymour to Drax. When I arrived at the site, the fog was very thick and I thought that was it for the day; however, as the sun rose higher, it partially burnt off the mist and this was the result.

By the time 7H18 was loaded, the mist had gone to leave a brilliantly sunny day. As I was waiting for the train to leave, 58005 *Ironbridge Power Station* appeared and was seen passing Seymour running as 6K68 from Worksop with empties to Oxcroft, as 56038 *Western Mail* waits to depart Seymour stock site line with 7H18 for Drax on 25 January 1997.

The final train from the stock site should have run on 28 January 1997, being hauled by 56089, which is seen setting back into the stock site with 6R84 from Milford Sidings. Passing on the main line is 58012, which was working 7B67 Oxcroft to West Burton power station.

With the few scrapings of remaining coal on the left, 56089 is now loading 7H12 Seymour to Drax power station and was projected to be the final train out of the stock site. It left at 3.02 p.m. on 28 January 1997 and just as expected did not prove to be the final train.

Just over a year later and after finding yet more coal, operations began again for a short period. Here Loadhaul-liveried 56109 is waiting for the last wagons to be loaded of 7F86 for Cottam power station at Seymour stock site on 16 March 1998.

The final few days saw a change of traction when 58050 was diagrammed to work into the site. Here, it loads an unidentified working at Seymour stocking site on 22 March 1998. This was my final visit to the stock site.

Bolsover Coalite

Closed in 1993, Bolsover Colliery latterly produced an annual output of 850,000 tons, much of which was used by the adjacent Coalite plant. After the colliery's closure, the Seymour Junction to Bolsover line remained open to serve the Coalite plant, with coal from collieries such as Kiveton, Gascoigne Wood, and Bevercotes.

In 1926, the Low Temperature Carbonisation Ltd (LTC) erected the Bolsover Coalite plant at the colliery to produce Coalite; then in 1936, the Derbyshire Coalite Company Ltd erected eight batteries of retorts to produce Coalite on a site to the west of Bolsover colliery. Production began in November 1936 using 500 tons of coal per day from the adjacent colliery. In 1938, the British Diesel Oil and Petrol Co. Ltd opened a chemical works on an adjacent site to refine the liquid products arising from the treatment of coal by the Coalite process. Full production was reached by 1939.

Renamed Coalite and Chemical Products Ltd in 1948, they continued to operate the Bolsover site through two subsidiaries—Derbyshire Coalite Co. Ltd, responsible for the smokeless fuel plant, and the British Diesel Oil and Petrol Co. Ltd, which ran the distillation plant, refinery, and chemical works. Coalite and Chemical Products Ltd was absorbed into Charrington Industrial Holdings Ltd in 1978, and in 1981, the group, now Coalite Group PLC, reorganised into Coalite Fuels and Chemical Ltd, which took over the Coalite plants at Bolsover, Askern, and Grimethorpe and the refinery at Bolsover.

Taken over by Anglo-United in 1989, in April 2004, Coalite Products Ltd appointed the receivers and the business closed in September 2004.

By the time I began photographing the area, coal was mostly obtained from Gascoigne Wood and Kiveton Park Colliery. The Gascoigne Wood empty wagons originated at Worksop as 6Y47 on the 11.23 p.m. to Gas Wood (as everyone knew it), travelling via the South Yorkshire Joint Line to Doncaster and Milford to wait time, before moving to Gascoigne Wood loading point. After loading, it ran as 6Y50 on the 4.14 a.m. to Bolsover via Moorthorpe, Swinton, and the Old Road to Foxlow Junction, arriving at Hall Lane Junction to await the opening of Seymour Junction 'box at about 5.30 a.m., in order to receive the train staff for the Bolsover branch.

Passing the Coalite Works, the driver would stop to drop off the train preparer (TP) at the ground frame, then pull forwards past the points. Using the Annett's key on the staff to unlock the ground frame, the TP would set the route into the plant. Calling the driver back, the train would be set back so far before stopping for the TP to uncouple the wagons.

The layout at Bolsover was just five short roads, so a consist of thirty-six HAAs would be split into three sets of twelve wagons and usually placed on Nos 1, 3, and 5 roads, ensuring they were just clear so the internal shunting loco could collect them—the curvature on No. 2 road prevented use by BR locomotives. Once all the wagons were in, the loco would return light to Worksop as 0Y50. Later that day, it would return to Bolsover as 0Y50 to collect the empty wagons, arriving at Bolsover at around 6 p.m.

The method of removal was different as the train would now have to be remade. According to one Worksop-based TP, 'the shunters weren't, let's say, helpful!' As the works shunter had isolated all the wagon brakes to allow their loco to move the wagons, and turned the 'Instanter' coupling from the short to long position, this all had to be reversed to allow the wagons to travel on the main line again. With the wagons coupled up and shunted into one train again, the train would head into the run-round loop, on the site of the long-closed Bolsover Castle station. The first set of points were hand points, and the second set were spring points. The TP says, 'We would run round as quick as possible because the little darling kids used to be a pain!'

After the run-round, the TP would couple the loco on the other end of the train and then move the train ASAP, back to the ground frame. Here, he would set the route back towards Seymour and draw the train forward for a brake test, then (and only then) put the tail lamp on and walk up to the loco, the reasoning being the tail lamp would be safe now as no one went near Coalite because of the smell. The train would return as 6Y42 7.04 p.m. to Worksop Upside. If the wagon set did not have any cripples (i.e. if any doors were still down), where possible, the same set would be used all week until planned preventative maintenance (PPM) dates expired.

The ex-Kiveton traffic would primarily consist of HEA wagons, again originating from Worksop to run empty to Kiveton. After loading as either 6T27, 6Y40, or 6Y42, the train would head to Woodhouse Junction to run around, then set off via Beighton Junction and Foxlow Junction towards Seymour, the method of working then being the same as the Gascoigne Wood trains. This service was photographed several times in different locations.

Worksop would often send any available loco to collect the empties, such as 37097 on 6T27 on 16 August 1995, and 47315 was obtained and used for a period on the Coalite traffic, being photographed on 6Y42 at the plant on 21 August 1996.

Bolsover also produced export Coalite for Ireland, via Seaforth. This utilised either MEAs or PFAs carrying Cawoods coal containers. On 28 June 2000, 56007 was photographed shunting 6G95 Bolsover to Healey Mills with MEAs. EWS served the

Coalite plant into the early 2000s, and my final photo of Bolsover was taken on 20 July 2000, when 58025 departed as 6Y42 at 7.04 p.m. for Worksop.

Freightliner reportedly ran a trial load of coal from Killoch in approximately August 2003, but word was that, on arrival, the train suffered a minor derailment due to the condition of track, and no more trains followed after that. Bolsover Coalite Chemicals Ltd went into administration, then receivership, and finally closed down in 2004.

Beginning the journey to Bolsover, 58010 is seen leaving Kiveton Colliery with 6T67 for Bolsover Coalite on 19 January 1994.

Arriving at Woodhouse Junction with 6Y40 Kiveton to Bolsover Coalite on 31 May 1994, 58030 enters the sidings where it will run round and then take the line towards Beighton and join the 'Old Road' at Beighton Junction. It will then take that route as far as Foxlow Junction, where it will diverge and take the route towards Seymour.

No. 58012 rounds the curve at Staveley with 6K67 Worksop to Oxcroft on 28 January 1997. The train is seen passing the site of the connection to the GCR main line and the Arkwright colliery branch, which was where the piles of ballast are in the image. This short-lived connection was put in to allow trains for Arkwright Colliery to avoid several run-round moves. However, the colliery closed not long after installation.

For a period in 1995, a selection of more unusual locos than the regular Class 56 and Class 58s were turned out from Worksop to work the Coalite traffic. Having deposited its loaded wagons at the Coalite plant and now returning to Worksop with an empty set, 37097 is seen passing under the former Great Central Main Line bridge at Staveley with 6T27 Bolsover Coalite to Worksop on 16 August 1995.

Having just accepted the staff for the Bolsover branch, 58031 now passes Seymour box with 6Y48 Kiveton Colliery to Bolsover Coalite on 26 May 1994.

Above: With the Coalite chemicals plant on the horizon, 58030 is passing the closed Markham Colliery with 6T67 return empties from Bolsover to Worksop on 31 May 1994.

Below: Taken from the other side of the line and from off the M1 Motorway overbridge, 58032 works 6T27 Bolsover Coalite to Worksop empties and passes the former entrance to Markham colliery on 8 August 1995. The loco is showing signs of its original red solebar livery.

We are now further along the branch, and this image was taken from a disused bridge once used by trucks taking spoil from Markham Colliery to the spoil heap opposite. Here, we see 56050 *British Steel Teesside* with 6Y42 Bolsover to Worksop on 26 July 1999, with the tanks and smoke stacks of the chemicals plant on the hillside.

Now we see the Coalite plant, and having arrived from Kiveton Colliery on 26 September 1994, 58028 has split its train into the sidings, these not being long enough to accommodate the whole train in one. Once the train had been shunted, the loco would return to Worksop light engine and then the internal Sentinel shunter will move the wagons a few at a time to the discharge area.

The Coalite internal Sentinel shunter begins its work and is seen here on 26 September 1994. The small shed on the right contains the ground frame, which works the points into the Coalite plant.

Having arrived from Worksop light loco, 47315 now sets to collecting the HAA wagons from the sidings to form 6Y42 7.04 p.m. to Worksop upside on 21 August 1996.

5

Yorkshire Area Collieries

'God's Own Country', as declared by a true Yorkshireman, had a large coalfield that stretched from Leeds in the north to Sheffield in the south, almost to Halifax on the west side and to Selby in the east. The Barnsley area was at the epicentre, but by the time I started taking photos, most of the collieries had gone. In this chapter, we begin with the Doncaster area.

Bentley

Coal was first found at Bentley Colliery, just north of Doncaster, when a bore hole was sunk to a depth of 615 yards to the 9-foot-thick Daw Wood seam, by the Vivian Boring Co. in 1893. In March 1902, Messrs Barber-Walker and Co. Ltd leased a large area from Sir William Cooke to sink shafts to the Barnsley Seam. Work began on the surface buildings in 1903, and the sinking of No. 2 shaft commenced on 9 October 1905. Due to certain issues, however, the sinking was abandoned, and instead, a new site was chosen 200 yards to the west. Work started in March 1906; shaft-sinking commenced on 22 September, with completion in 1908 when headings were being driven out from the pit bottom. To serve the pit, a new triangular rail link was made to the Doncaster to York line (about half a mile to the east) together with a connection to the Hull and Barnsley line at the other end of the colliery.

In 1932, No. 2 shaft was sunk a further 216 yards to gain the Parkgate and Thorncliffe seams, to complement the Barnsley and Dunsil seams already being worked. The latter seams were further developed during the war, and by the late 1950s, they were providing about one-third of the total output.

The pit was modernised in 1939 when flame-proof diesel locomotives were introduced underground for moving men and coal. By 1945, mechanical working

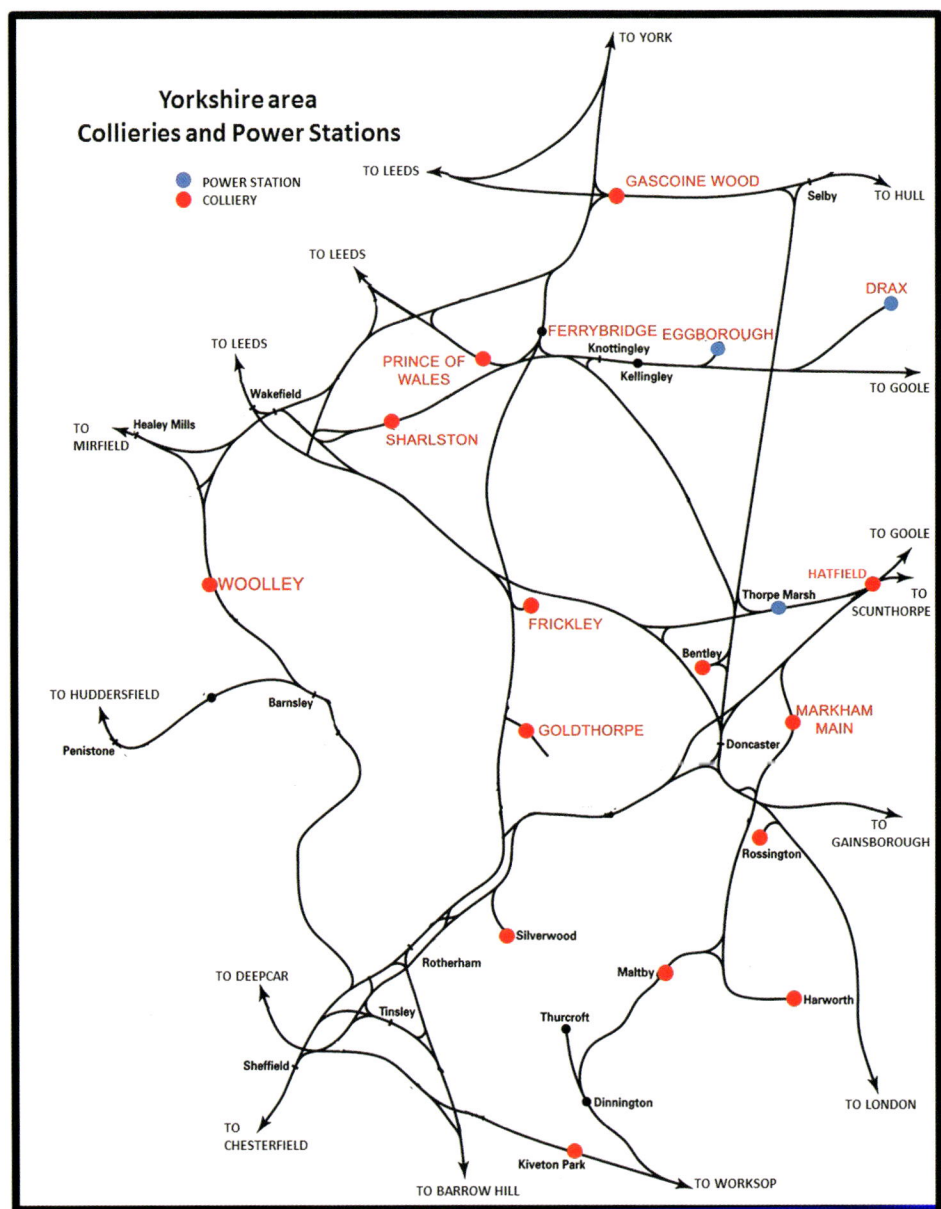

Yorkshire area map. The coloured dots are locations photographed.

of the seams took over. Skip winding and conveyor systems were introduced in the 1960s, but a fire in the Barnsley seam during the strike of 1974 led to the north-east district being sealed off and lost. The Dunsil seam would continue being worked, and between 1975 and 1982, drifts were put into a new area of Barnsley coal near Thorpe Marsh power station, after which output came entirely from the Dunsil seam until it was exhausted in 1984. The Barnsley seam was still being worked in 1983 until it too was exhausted in 1988.

A rapid-loading bunker was commissioned on 9 July 1976 and all other sidings dispensed with. Further development on the Sallow Wood seam had begun in 1980, which produced coal two years later, and the Parkgate seam was gained in 1987.

British Coal announced its intention to close Bentley Colliery on 16 November 1993, quoting low prices that had led to a lack of markets for its coal. It closed on 3 December 1993 with a loss of 450 jobs. The colliery was demolished during late 1994–early 1995.

I only ever made two visits to Bentley, both after the closure and demolition of the surface buildings, including the rapid-loading bunker, and when the remaining coal stocks were being removed via a temporary pad-loading area. Access to view the train was gained by leaving the car next to the level crossing at Shaftholme Road (on the East Coast Main Line), then walking along a disused road that once went beneath the line, as far as the point where it was blocked. It was then a scramble alongside the railway down to the west-to-north curve of the colliery access line and onto the former colliery site.

A Loadhaul-liveried Class 56 was being loaded, and no one batted an eyelid about my being there to photograph it. It was a freezing cold and dull 6 December 1995,

On a very dull and freezing cold December day, I was the only person around to photograph 56100, which was about ready to depart from the former Bentley colliery site after loading 7C06 for Ferrybridge power station on 6 December 1995.

A second view of 56100 as it now departs for Ferrybridge power station and takes the west to north curve on 6 December 1995. When the pit was in operation, this view would have included the rapid loading bunker at the far end of the train, this being swept away along with the colliery in 1994.

The second visit to the site was on a sunny but still very cold 29 February 1996, the sea of mud still being frozen. Here the driver of Trainload Coal sector 56126 waits patiently as two mechanical shovels load his train, which will form 7H10 for Drax.

Again taken on 29 February 1996, 56126 takes 7H10 for Drax on to the west to north curve towards the connection with the East Coast Main Line; the rusty rails of the south to west curve testify to the lack of use as all trains were sent northwards to either Ferrybridge or Drax.

and the thick colliery waste was fortunately frozen solid; I think the driver must have looked at me and thought I was mad.

I returned to the site two months later for my final visit in order to obtain a photo in better weather conditions. Although the sun was out, the mud was still frozen, which was a bonus. This time, I obtained a shot of the Class 56 while being loaded and departing the site. Today, the track beds of the access curves can still be seen from trains passing on the ECML, but the mud and colliery waste have gone and the site was redeveloped in 1998 into a nature area, forming part of the Bentley community forest.

Frickley-South Elmsall

Frickley Colliery was situated 10 miles north-west of Doncaster and 7 miles south of Pontefract, on the edge of the village of South Elmsall in West Yorkshire. The first sod was cut by the Carlton Main Colliery Company on 28 April 1903, with two 23-foot-diameter shafts sunk. The Barnsley seam was hit on 23 May 1905 at a depth of 662 yards, and both shafts were later deepened to the Dunsil seam at a depth of 682 yards.

The Frickley name stems from the colliery being sunk within the land of Frickley Hall, part of the small hamlet of Frickley. The colliery was built adjacent to the Swinton and Knottingley Joint line between Thurnscoe and Moorthorpe, and in 1908, a contract was let to widen the then-single line railway between Moorthorpe and the colliery to two running lines. A second connection was also made to the Hull

& Barnsley & West Riding Junction Railway's Wath branch between Wrangbrook Junction and Wath.

In April 1920, intermittent work started on sinking a third 14-foot-diameter shaft. This reached the Shafton seam at a depth of 238 yards in November 1923. No. 3 shaft was treated as a separate colliery called South Elmsall, but it relied on Frickley's No. 2 shaft for upcast.

Production ceased in the Shafton seam in 1925, and the Barnsley seam was worked until 1942 when the Dunsil seam was entered, although coal winding remained at the original Barnsley level. By 1927, the output from Frickley was reported as 23,000 tons a week, with South Elmsall producing 10,000 tons a week. Pit head baths were opened on 19 March 1938, and in that year, 1,013,640 tons were produced. On vesting day, 1 January 1947, the colliery became part of NCB North Eastern Division No. 4 Carlton Area Sub Area 'A', later becoming part of the Doncaster Area Group 'C' in 1965. Work continued at South Elmsall until 1966, when it was closed as the Shafton seam was exhausted, and the mines were merged in 1968 as Frickley-South Elmsall.

Modernisation in June 1968 saw the installation of a £400,000 rapid-loading bunker for MGR trains with a capacity of 2,300 tons. This could load a 1,000-ton train in twenty-five minutes with a total turnaround time of sixty minutes. The year 1970 saw the Cudworth seam replace the Shafton seam, and in 1984, the Top Haigh Moor seam replaced the Barnsley seam. After the 1984–1985 miners' strike, the colliery became part of British Coal South Yorkshire area, but manpower was down to 1,393. In 1986, the Dunsil seam ceased production, and another transfer in 1990 saw the colliery become part of the North Yorkshire Group.

In the financial year ending March 1992, production was at 1,057,000 tons. That August saw production commence in the Newhill seam, but in October, Frickley-South Elmsall was one of the thirty-one collieries intended for closure. It was granted a thirteen-month reprieve while studies showed it was one of British Coal's most profitable collieries, and in 1993, it became part of the Northern Group.

Prior to its closure, Frickley was sending trains to Ferrybridge 'C' power station with departures at 3.11 p.m. on Thursday and Fridays only, and at 7.47 p.m. Saturdays excepted. With no market or contract to supply any of the electricity generators in 1993, and only 8 per cent of the output destined for industrial and coking purposes, by the end of September 1993, there was a coal stockpile of 269,000 tons.

The 735 miners were forced to vote on closure in November 1993. Despite having plentiful and easily accessible reserves, the colliery closed on 26 November. Like other collieries, Frickley was swiftly demolished, leaving behind large coal stockpiles to be removed. The first train out of the colliery post-demolition was in December 1996; most of the stockpiled coal was destined for Drax power station. With no run-round facilities, trains were top and tailed. On my first visit to observe operations on 17 January 1997, I photographed 56126 in the loading area. A second visit was made on 23 April 1997 to see 56006 and 56052 on the train. Since then, new housing has sprung up, and a 180-acre country park now occupies the site.

After the demolition of Frickley Colliery, the operation to remove the coal stocks involved trains being top and tailed as there were no run-round facilities. Here on 17 January 1997, 56126 is at the rear of 7H13, which is almost loaded and will depart from Frickley to Drax.

A higher view of the loading area surrounded by heaps of coal in different processing areas. No. 56126 is at the rear of the train with the train engine out of view around the curve. Two mechanical shovels load the train with just three wagons left to load.

A view of 56052 at the head of the train, with 56006 at the far end having just arrived with 6F27 from Milford. Loading of the first wagon has just begun, which formed 7H11 for Drax on 23 April 1997.

Having been to Drax and returned to Frickley to form the afternoon working out, 56052 is now at the rear of 7H10 Frickley to Drax as it is entering the loop at Moorthorpe. Here the train will stop and reverse back towards the camera, making the second train of the day to Drax on 23 April 1997.

Gascoigne Wood

The Selby coalfield in North Yorkshire would become the largest deep-mining complex in the world. There were five interconnecting deep mines at Wistow, Stillingfleet, Riccall, North Selby, and Whitemoor, with the ten shafts linking to more than 400 miles of underground roadways. All the coal was brought to the surface via twin drift shafts at Gascoigne Wood. It took twenty years and £1.3 billion to bring the complex into production; the first coal was mined at Wistow in June 1983 and sent to Gascoigne Wood for onwards distribution by rail.

The rail complex was situated on both sides of the Leeds to Hull line and was formerly a North Eastern Railway marshalling yard. It was extended to allow access from the west end via Milford Junction (on the Wakefield to York route) or from the east end from the Hull line or the ECML at Hambleton Junction.

Within the complex, there were two 30-m high bunkers side-by-side, each with a capacity of 3,000 tons. A control room was situated between the bunkers. A third bunker for the removal of spoil was also provided, situated to one side of the other two bunkers. Additionally, there was a discharge facility on the Up side to allow coal to be brought in for blending. Original plans were for trains to be loaded around the clock at a rate of one every twenty-three minutes for onward movement to the Aire and Trent Valley power stations.

The Gascoigne Wood complex was privatised in the early 1990s and was owned by RJB Mining, later UK Coal. Selby never quite fulfilled its promise, and only once (in 1993–94) did it achieve its planned annual output of 12 million tons. Some 121 million tons were mined in total, but due to the low price of coal and the reluctance to open up difficult areas of the coal measures, millions of tons more of resources were deemed uneconomic and were left untouched. Four of the mines were merged into two in the late 1990s to reduce costs, but the costs of the central depot at Gascoigne Wood could not be supported by the three pits, and the closure of the complex was announced in 2002. Production was planned to be run down over the next few years, but in 2004, the whole complex was closed and the shafts filled. Although the sidings remain today, the coal loading bunkers were demolished leaving just the control room standing. Recently the site has been used for dealing with gypsum created by the power stations, and for the storage of off-lease rolling stock.

Back in the 1990s, Gascoigne Wood was a hive of activity day and night with trains arriving and departing at regular intervals, although not quite to the twenty-three-minute timetable originally envisaged. As the loading area was out of bounds, the next nearest vantage point was Milford Junction. On one occasion, however, I did manage a close-up view from the west end of the complex. Other views were available at the east end from a level crossing on Common Lane.

The one and only time I got this close to the area sees busy scene at the Gascoigne Wood complex in which 58009, 56135, 56077, and 56035 are being loaded on 6 September 1994.

After loading, 56035 wearing construction sector markings is now departing Selby with 7R87 to Drax on 6 September 1994.

The last-built Class 56, 56135 *Port of Tyne Authority*, passes Gascoigne Wood signal box as it leaves with 7G43 to Tees Yard on 6 September 1994.

As viewed from the signal box, 56088 is passing Gascoigne Wood main line with 7H19 Thorpe Marsh power station to Milford Sidings on 6 September 1994. This was after the closure of Thorpe Marsh power station and during the period coal stocks were being removed, as will be explained in Chapter 7.

As viewed from the access road to the loading complex at Gascoigne Wood, National Power 59204 *Vale of Glamorgan* departs from with a loaded train for Drax on 8 June 1997.

National Power sold its rail assets to EWS in April 1998 and the Class 59s were soon repainted into EWS livery. In the same location and just over one year from the previous photo here is 59204 *Vale of Glamorgan* in its new guise but still hauling a rake of blue JMAs for Drax on 30 October 1998.

A little further around the curve from Gascoigne Wood and as viewed from the Common Lane overbridge, 59202 *Vale of White Horse* heads round the curve towards Milford with another load of the 'black stuff' for Drax power station on 30 October 1998.

Goldthorpe

Henry Lodge Ltd began sinking two shafts for a new Goldthorpe colliery soon after the construction of the Dearne Valley Railway, with the first sod cut on 29 July 1909. Initially worked by pillar and stall methods, longwall methods were introduced in 1950, and the increased output necessitated a new drift, driven from the surface to the Shafton seam between 1956 and January 1958.

In 1966, Goldthorpe was linked underground with Highgate and began winding the latter's coal. The two were treated as a single mine, called 'Goldthorpe–Highgate', from 1967 to 1985. A new return drift was driven from Hickleton pit yard into the combined workings, and the Highgate workings were closed in 1985. On 1 January 1986, Goldthorpe and Hickleton were merged to become 'Goldthorpe–Hickleton'.

A new 3,000-ton capacity rapid-loading bunker was opened at Goldthorpe in September 1968, situated on the remaining stretch of the Dearne Valley Railway from a connection to the Swinton and Knottingley line, south of Thurnscoe station. Although on the list of mines to be retained, Goldthorpe was closed on 4 February 1994 and placed on 'care and maintenance'.

Unfortunately, the coal reserves were judged too small and, with no buyer found, the mine closed in October 1994. It had been demolished by April 1995, despite having easily accessible reserves of 5 million tons.

Despite several attempts to obtain a photograph at Goldthorpe, I was only ever actually able to get a photo of it once. On the first occasion, I was without a map (in those days before smart phones and map apps) and was unable to find a spot for a photo. On the second and third attempts, I had found a vantage point looking east from the B6098 High Street Bridge, but the trains were cancelled. It was only on the

Above left: No. 58007 is seen making a very smoky departure from the bunker at Goldthorpe with 7G42 on the 8.55 a.m. Goldthorpe to West Burton on 17 June 1993.

Above right: A second shot of 58007 departing from the bunker at Goldthorpe with 7G42 on the 8.55 a.m. Goldthorpe to West Burton on 17 June 1993.

fourth attempt that I managed to get a shot of a train. After closure of the colliery, the Goldthorpe colliery branch was abandoned. The signalling from the main line to the colliery was abolished on 22 November 1998.

Hatfield

The Hatfield Main Colliery Co. Ltd chose to sink a colliery on a site next to the GCR's Doncaster to Scunthorpe line, and the first sod was cut to begin shaft-sinking on 14 October 1911. Two 6.7-m-diameter shafts were sunk simultaneously, No. 1 shaft reaching the Barnsley seam at a depth of 860 yards in August 1916. Issues with water influx meant that No. 2 shaft was not finished until 1917. The colliery was also linked via a railway to staithes on the Sheffield and South Yorkshire Navigation.

Coal production from the Barnsley seam, which was up to 10 feet thick in places, began in 1917 and continued until 1983. The 4-foot-thick Kent's thick seam was worked between 1917 and 1922; thereafter, subsequent work was confined to the Barnsley seam.

In January 1927, Hatfield was incorporated into the Carlton Main Colliery Company, and work began on the High Hazels seam. This seam of high-quality coal was around 4 feet thick and was worked until 2004.

Hatfield merged with Thorne colliery in 1967, although the latter remained mothballed. They were separated in 1978, when it was proposed to redevelop Thorne, but merged again in 1986 when that project was abandoned. A new £450,000 rapid-loading bunker was opened in July 1971.

British Coal stopped production on 3 December 1993, but, in a management buyout, the Hatfield Coal Co. Ltd was incorporated on 25 January 1993. British Coal cut its last coal in the High Hazels seam on 7 March 1994, and the new company cut its first coal on 7 July 1994. A profit of £2.4 million was made in the first year, but geological problems in 2000 cut the planned output by a fifth from 500,000 tons *per annum*. Although operating aid was sought from the government, this did not prevent the company going into receivership, and the mine was closed on 9 August 2001.

The site was mothballed, with funding from the department of trade and industry, until October when Coalpower Ltd, run by Richard J. Budge (the former owner of RJB Mining), took control of the pit. In 2003, the company published plans for a 33-hectare 'Power Park'. This would include a 450-MW power station at the site, but geological problems at the coal face led to losses. In late 2003, Coalpower went into administration and Hatfield closed in early 2004.

The doubling of coal prices between 2004 and 2008 saw Richard J. Budge form a company entitled Powerfuel to take on the colliery in 2006, and Russian coal company Kuzbassrazrezugol (KRU) took a 51-per cent stake in the venture and coal production began in March 2007.

Plans for a carbon capture and storage (CCS) coal-burning power station at the site were announced, and although £180 million of EU funding was approved in 2009, the venture came to nought. In December 2010, in part due to coal production problems, Powerfuel Mining Ltd entered administration.

That was still not the end of the story as in 2011, 2Co Energy Ltd acquired the company and renamed it Hatfield Colliery Ltd. It planned to continue the CCS project, which it renamed 'Don Valley Power Project'. The colliery was then managed under contract by Hargreaves Services Plc, which was then working Maltby Colliery. An employee-controlled company, Hatfield Colliery Partnership Limited (HCPL), purchased the mine from ING Bank in December 2013. A bridging loan of £4 million from the National Union of Mineworkers, in September 2014, allowed production to be moved to a new pit face. This was intended to extend mining until summer 2016, but coal production at Hatfield ended on 29 June 2015. Work on filling the shafts began in August 2015.

I was a latecomer to photographing Hatfield and, as such, took few photographs that fit within the time period of this book. My first visit was on 19 May 1999, and while a few more shots were taken that year, in the main, my photos of the colliery are from 2000 onwards, up until its closure. I wish sometimes that I had made the effort much earlier, particularly to see the many semaphore signals in the area before the opening of Doncaster power box and the operation of the rapid-loading bunker at Hatfield. The bunker was originally worked on the slip train process, whereby a train of empty wagons would arrive and the loco would be uncoupled, to be coupled to a previously-loaded full set for onward movement to the power station. The empty set

Above: As viewed from a footpath crossing (once Bootham Lane level crossing, leading to the long gone Bootham Farm), 58007 *Drakelow Power Station* is seen beneath the rapid-loading bunker at Hatfield Colliery on 2 August 1996. The train was 7B68 Hatfield Colliery to West Burton and was only the second train out of the colliery after being taken over by the Hatfield Coal Co. Ltd in July 1994.

Below: After loading the wagons and running around the train, 58007 *Drakelow Power Station* now pulls back through the bunker to top up top up the wagons and make 7B68 to West Burton on 2 August 1996.

would be pulled through the bunker via a cable-worked 'mule', which was kept in its 'garage' close to the bunker. The machine worked via an endless cable attached to a motor, which pulled the mule out of its garage and to the rear of the empty wagons. The mule would be attached to the wagons and then pulled back towards its garage, thus pulling the wagons beneath the loading bunker. By the time they were loaded, another train had arrived and the cycle continued. To prevent the mule coming out of its garage and the cable being run over by a moving train, the system was interlocked with Doncaster PSB so that a release had to be requested by the bunker operator. Although the mule was out of use by the late 1980s, it was still in its garage when the mine closed for the final time.

Loading complete, 58007 *Drakelow Power Station* now departs from Hatfield Colliery with 7B68 for West Burton on 2 August 1996.

Above: We are now looking eastwards from the Station Road overbridge, and 58024 is departing from Hatfield Colliery with 7F94 the 4.55 p.m. for Cottam on 18 June 1999.

Right: As viewed from the footbridge of Stainforth and Hatfield station, 58019 *Shirebrook Colliery* departs from Hatfield Colliery with 7F94 for Cottam power station as 37219 approaches in background on 19 May 1999.

Kiveton

At the time that the Kiveton Park Coal Co. Ltd was formed in March 1864, the rural village of the same name consisted of nothing more than a dozen farm houses. The site was chosen as it was adjacent to the 1849-opened Sheffield and Lincolnshire Junction Railway (a constituent part of the Manchester, Sheffield and Lincolnshire Railway), thus allowing both easy transportation of materials to the colliery and an outlet for the coal.

Sinking at Kiveton Park began on 6 June 1866, and on 5 December 1867, the Barnsley seam was reached at a depth of 405 yards. This shaft was later deepened to 670 yards to access the 3-foot 8-inch-thick Thorncliffe seam, the coal of which was used for coking; coke ovens were built at the colliery for the purpose. The colliery offices were built in 1875, doubling as a school as there was no such facility in the district.

As the Thorncliffe seam contained a layer of dirt, it could not be economically worked and was therefore abandoned in 1896. At the same time, another shaft was sunk adjacent to the Barnsley seam and was connected to it. For ventilation purposes, the shaft was sunk further down to the Silkstone seam at a depth of 733 yards. This shaft also passed the High Hazels seam at a depth of 310 yards, and coal production commenced in 1900.

Purely for business reasons, Kiveton Park Colliery was amalgamated with Sherwood Colliery in 1928, and the colliery was taken over by the United Steel Co. in 1944. The coal was hand-won until 1929, when mechanical coal cutters and conveyors were introduced into the Barnsley seam in 1932. By 1940, all hand-working was superseded by machinery, and power loading was introduced in 1944. Prior to the machine age, 67 per cent of the output was large lumps of coal and used for locos, shipping, and household purposes, while the small coal was used for manufacturing purposes.

By the 1960s, the colliery had an annual average output of between 500,000–600,000 tons; while the tonnage did not vary greatly over the years, the number of men required to produce that amount had halved. In April 1929, the colliery's highest employment figure was reached at 2,244, but by 1967, this had reduced to 1,054 men, employed as follows: 416 (coalface), 405 (others underground), and 233 (surface).

By 1967, the percentage of large coal was never more than 20 per cent as a result of total mechanisation. A typical week's saleable output was 10,000 tons, of which 7,500 tons was small coal destined for power stations, 500 tons of Barnsley cobble coal for locos, and the remainder High Hazels cobble coal for the domestic market, chiefly around Manchester. The Barnsley seam, which was exhausted in 1970, varied in thickness between 4 feet and 5 feet 6 inches, while the High Hazels seam had a maximum thickness of 4 feet.

With no space at Kiveton Park to erect a rapid-loading bunker, a new 4,000-ton capacity loading pad was constructed in 1989.

Production and productivity figures for the final week before closure showed that a target output of 13,200 tons had been exceeded and was standing at 18,085, a gain of 4,885 tons. Output for the year was standing at 384,121 with a target of 500,000 tons; to achieve the annual target, an average output per week was set at 16,554 tons. That target was never achieved as the last shift worked on 30 September 1994. A skeleton workforce and contractors were brought in to close and demolish the colliery after almost 130 years of production.

The last train to leave the intact colliery ran as 7K03 on the 3.50 p.m. Kiveton to Worksop Yard on 25 November 1994, hauled by 58012. The operation to remove the accumulated stockpiles began almost immediately after closure, even continuing as the colliery succumbed to the demolition crews.

I returned to the colliery as often as I could, but my final Kiveton Park photo was taken on 12 May 1995. Trains ended five days later, not long after locals gathered to watch the headgear being pulled down. Since then, the site has been cleared and is now part of a fishing lake complex. Only the original office buildings remain to serve as a reminder of the past.

Kiveton Colliery from the east end as viewed from the Hard Lane overbridge, and 58035 is just about ready to depart Kiveton Colliery with 7G33 for West Burton power station on 10 June 1994. The green area was once part of the empty sidings for the colliery, these being dispensed with when pad-loaded MGR operations began.

After snowfall, 58040 *Cottam Power Station* is seen at the west end of the colliery loading 7G34 for West Burton on 26 January 1995. The train has arrived from Worksop and pulled past the loading pad where the rear end is being loaded adjacent to the pad. As the wagons are loaded, the train will be pushed away from the camera, and once loading is completed, the loco will detach, run out of the colliery onto the down main line, then run facing road to the other end of the colliery where it will then leave the main line and enter the colliery at the east end. It will then be recoupled to the other end of its train and be made ready to depart.

No. 58040 *Cottam Power Station* loading 7G34 at Kiveton Colliery is now viewed from the platform of Kiveton Bridge station on 26 January 1995.

No. 58001 prepares to depart Kiveton Colliery after loading 7F08 for Cottam power station on 25 April 1995.

As limestone begins to arrive to fill the shafts of the now-closed colliery, 58010 makes a smoky departure from Kiveton Colliery with 7G34 for West Burton, on Thursday, 9 February 1995.

Maltby

The Maltby Main Colliery Company, a subsidiary of the Sheepbridge Iron and Coal Company, sank the first shafts at Maltby Main Colliery on 30 March 1908. The Barnsley seam was reached at 820 yards on 17 June 1910. Production was underway by 1912, and the mine was producing 1 million tons *per annum* by the mid-1930s.

The Barnsley seam would remain in production until 1972, but deepening of the two shafts allowed access to a new Swallow Wood seam, which commenced production after the Barnsley seam was considered exhausted. A rapid-loading bunker was built in the mid-1970s, although pad loading was also undertaken in the sidings.

Sinking of a third shaft started in October 1982 in a major £180 million project to mine the Parkgate seam, at a depth of 1,115 yards. Completed in November 1989, production from the seam began in 1992.

British Coal ceased production temporarily in May 1993, placing the mine on development-only status. Following privatisation, the colliery was purchased in 1994 by RJB Mining. Maltby also took over the reserves of the closed Silverwood Colliery, but due to uncertainties with contracts for the outlet of coal, production ceased in 1997. The pit did, however, restart operations, and coal was gained from both the Parkgate and Silkstone seams.

UK Coal sold the colliery to Hargreaves Services plc for £21.5 million in 2007, the coal being intended for their coking plant at Monkton.

In 2013, a new development to be exploited on T125 face was halted when oil, water, and gas seeped into the tailgate, forcing abandonment. A tailgate is a return roadway/airway, usually where materials were transported to the coal face, whereas the maingate was the intake roadway/airway to the coal face. The word 'gate' means roadway and is nothing to do with actual gates.

This was expected only to cause a gap in production of up to three months, but faced with huge losses, in December 2012, the 540 employees were given redundancy notices instead, and Hargreaves announced it would mothball the colliery. The mine closed in 2013 with demolition following soon after. No. 3 winding tower was blown up at 1.15 p.m. on 16 July 2014.

Despite Maltby being close to my home, and my having worked with trains destined for the colliery for twenty years, I had never photographed trains at the colliery until on one sunny day in June 1995, when I decided to chance my luck. I drove into the colliery and went to the admin offices to seek permission to photograph a train as it was loading. After speaking to the receptionist, she went into an office and spoke to the manager, Mr Clive Ponder, who surprisingly agreed. Permission was granted on condition that I wore safety boots (check), a hi-vis coat (check), and safety glasses (check), and that I was in possession of a personal track safety card (check). The final condition was that he wanted to see my photographs before any were released for publication, to which I agreed. The train I photographed was 7H33 for Drax, which, on the day in question, was hauled by 56089. Being given free reign meant I took several shots of the train during the loading process, some of which feature here.

With the film developed (no digital cameras back then), I returned to the colliery to show the images to the manager. He asked if I could get one of them enlarged so that he could hang it on his office wall, so I agreed and went off to get one done. A few days later, I returned with a 16 × 20-inch enlargement, suitably framed, which delighted the manager. He asked me about what I photographed, and would I be interested in a contract to photograph colliery equipment on the surface and below ground. If I had been equipped with a suitable camera and flash gun for below ground, I would have snatched his hand off, but batteries are classed as contraband in mines, so unfortunately, there was no way I could accept the offer.

October 1995 saw the first visit to Maltby by National Power Class 59 locos, when almost-new 59202 and 59205 top and tailed a train of JMA wagons into the colliery for weights and measures tests. This time, I was denied an access request and had to be content with shots close to the bunker line. I would return to Maltby on many further occasions to photograph, but my visits were mostly in the vicinity of Maltby Colliery South signal box. Following the colliery's demolition, I often wondered what became of the photo in Mr Ponder's office.

On the day of my visit to Maltby Colliery, 56089 waits at the ground position light on the bunker line to be given permission to proceed towards the rapid loading bunker, where it will load 7H33 for Drax power station on 7 June 1995. Notice the 10R banner repeater signal for No. 10 signal, which when in the 'off' position informs the driver that the route is set for him to come off the bunker line when the train is loaded. The lines to the left are part of the former loaded sidings.

The train is now pulling through the bunker and heading towards the buffer stops. It will then set back and begin loading as it propels through the bunker.

With the fan house to the right and conveyor systems behind, the train is still easing towards the buffer stops.

Maltby Colliery No. 3 upcast shaft headgear dominates the scene as the train sets back towards the bunker and is loaded to form 7H33 for Drax power station on 7 June 1995.

Before National Power could begin operations from Maltby Colliery, they had to carry out weight and measures testing. Here is 6G80 on the bunker line at Maltby Colliery on 16 October 1995. The train was top and tailed, and on the left is 59202 *Vale of White Horse* while leading the train was 59205 *Vale of Evesham*, which can be seen close to the bunker.

Leading the weights and measures train was 59205 *Vale of Evesham*. Here, it is close to the bunker. The lines in the foreground are part of the former colliery sidings, comprising of Nos 1 and 2 roads for empty wagons with nos 3, 4, 5, and 6 for loaded wagons.

Markham Main

Not to be confused with Markham Colliery in Derbyshire, Markham Main Colliery was situated in Armthorpe, on the eastern edge of Doncaster and adjacent to the South Yorkshire Joint Railway.

The story of Markham began in June 1913, when Earl Fitzwilliam leased the minerals under his Armthorpe estate to Sir Arthur Markham, in whose honour the colliery was named. Sinking two 17-foot-diameter shafts started on 16 May 1916, but this was discontinued on 24 August as the wartime conditions consumed the available manpower. Although work resumed in 1919, it was suspended again until 21 May 1922. Both reached the Barnsley seam in May 1924 at a depth of 731 yards.

The South Yorkshire Joint Railway connection allowed the coal to be transported northwards to the GCR's Doncaster to Barnetby line and onwards to Immingham for export, or to the south via Doncaster and Worksop.

Originally, the faces were worked entirely by hand, but in 1934, the first conveyor was introduced, and a coal-cutting machine was introduced in 1937, and the same year Markham Main was absorbed by the Doncaster Amalgamated Collieries Ltd, which worked the colliery until nationalisation in 1947. By June 1942, conveyors were taking coal from the faces and feeding it onto gate belts.

Under NCB ownership, the Dunsil seam was worked on the north-east side of the shafts between 1954–58, although where the Dunsil seam united with the Barnsley seam to give 14 feet of coal in other parts of the take, the full section was not worked. By now, the colliery was producing 14,000 tons a week, and prior to the miners' strike of 1984, this had risen to around 24,000 tons a week, with most of the production going to the Aire Valley and Trent Valley power stations. The workforce from Markham Main were the final Yorkshire miners to return to work, and at the end of the strike in 1985, they were soon producing 18,000 tons per week.

The NCB became the British Coal Corporation in 1987, but Markham Main was making losses. Despite its substantial reserves, it was closed on 16 October 1992. In 1993, the pit was described as 'non-operational', but it was reopened by Coal Investments Ltd in 1994. This company was headed by Malcolm Edwards, a former commercial director of British Coal, who took over the operation of six collieries.

The ground frame-operated rail connection from the South Yorkshire Joint Railway had been taken out of use after the mine's initial closure. However, the section of line from Markham Sidings ground frame (GF) to Markham Main was restored to use, and the first test train ran from the colliery to Eggborough power station on 29 March 1995. Sadly, operations were short-lived as Coal Investments went into administration in February 1996.

Unfortunately, a buyer could not be found for the colliery, and on 28 June 1996, ownership was handed by the liquidators to the Coal Authority. Markham Main required around £8 million of investment to improve a face gap in the coal seam, and as such, it was a less attractive prospect than other mines. Had the investment been found, it would have received firm contracts from National Power and Eastern Group. With the heavy losses continuing, Markham finally closed in September 1996.

Accessing the colliery for photos involved a walk through Sandall Beat Woods to a footbridge over the South Yorkshire Joint Line, adjacent to the GF. Here it was possible to see the trains arrive or depart, and my first foray to do so was on 1 February 1994 when the coal stockpiles were being removed. No. 56005 was in charge, propelling 7F32 on the 11.45 a.m. to Ferrybridge power station from the colliery to the run-round loop, then heading away south towards Doncaster. I only visited again in March and June 1994, but I have returned to the site since to find a pleasant park and housing estate.

This view of Markham Main Colliery is from a footbridge spanning the South Yorkshire Joint Line (bottom left) and the colliery sidings. No. 56005 propels 7F32 on the 11.45 a.m. Markham Main to Ferrybridge from the colliery to run the round loop, which is behind the camera on 1 February 1994.

Still propelling back into the run-round loop, 56005 makes smoky work of it. The South Yorkshire Joint Railway is on the right, and we are looking in the direction of Doncaster.

After running around, the loco now propels out of the colliery yard onto the South Yorkshire Joint Railway.

No. 56005 sets off towards Doncaster with 7F32 on the 11.45 a.m. Markham Main to Ferrybridge on 1 February 1994.

A closer view of the loading area at Markham Main Colliery as 56091 *Thorpe Marsh Power Station* is loading 7H19 to Drax power station on 3 March 1994. Just six wagons remain to load before the train is ready to depart.

Loading complete, 56091 *Thorpe Marsh Power Station* is now propelling into the run-round loop at Markham Main on 3 March 1994.

A view from the other side of the loading area as 56108 is loading 7H19 to Drax on 7 March 1994. The train is loaded and awaits the nod to set back towards the run-round loop.

No. 56108 is setting back with 7H19 to Drax on 7 March 1994. There seems to be an awful lot of coal yet to be graded for sending to the power stations.

Prince of Wales

Situated on the northern edge of Pontefract, an act of parliament in 1869 repealed the prohibition of coal working beneath Pontefract Park. As the Haigh seam had been accessed at nearby Glasshoughton Colliery, John Rhodes of Snydale Hall was minded to sink a colliery in Pontefract to access the same seam. He subsequently leased 1,044 acres of Haigh Moor coal from HRH Prince of Wales' duchy of Lancaster and 460 acres from the trustees of Pontefract Park. Although it was named Prince of Wales Colliery for the main land owner, it was rarely referred to as such and was generally referred to as 'Pontefract Colliery' or 'Pontie Pit' by the workforce.

Sinking of two 14-foot-diameter shafts was started close to the Lancashire and Yorkshire Railway's Methley branch on 21 June 1870. The Haigh Moor seam was reached at a depth of 461 yards on 24 July 1872, and its official opening was on 8 October 1874.

Although the colliery was producing the best-quality coal, the workers were laid off on 5 June 1875 due to a lack of demand. By 1882, work had resumed, and 500–600 tons were being produced daily. By 1896, 475 men and boys were employed underground, with eighty-one men on the surface.

Rhodes died in 1911, and the business became John Roads Limited, the colliery then employing 1,452 men. Sinking of a new 18-foot-diameter shaft was commenced in 1911 but not completed until 1925.

The 1926 strikes and the poor economic climate severely affected the pit. By 1928, it was in such a dire position that it was forced to close in July to reduce the coal stocks.

Work recommenced the following month, only to cease again that September. The loss of so many jobs in the locality led to Pontefract Town Council negotiating with the Glasshoughton and Castleford Collieries Company to purchase and reopen the colliery. Pontefract Collieries Ltd was therefore incorporated in November 1928, and the pit was purchased from John Roads Limited; it reopened on 7 December 1928.

A reconstruction of the pit was necessary due to its condition, but coal was soon produced from the Beeston and Silkstone seams. In 1930, the railway sidings were rearranged, and pit head baths with facilities for 2,000 men were opened in October 1933.

Upon nationalisation in January 1947, the colliery became part of the NCB North Eastern Division No. 8 Castleford Area Sub Area 'C' with a complement of 1,920 men. Coal was then being won from the Castleford four foot, Warren House, Haigh Moor, and Silkstone seams. The year 1958 saw the maximum number of men employed at the mine—a total of 2,200, working five seams. By 1971, there were 1,409 men, producing 660,000 tons of coal that year. June 1980 saw the construction of a 2,250-ton-capacity rapid-loading bunker.

Prince of Wales Colliery became part of the NCB New North Yorkshire area on 1 October 1985, and by financial year ending March 1989, it was employing 1,050 men who produced 1,500,000 tons of coal.

In late 1993, the colliery was sending out three trains per week to Drax. They arrived at the power station at 9.13 a.m. on Wednesdays, Thursdays, and Fridays only, at 4.23 p.m. on Sundays only, and at 9.03 p.m. on Mondays and Tuesdays only.

My one and only photo of a train at Prince of Wales Colliery is this one taken on 2 September 1994. Here, 56055 in Trainload Construction livery is leaving Prince of Wales Colliery with 7H20 for Drax power station and is passing Prince of Wales Colliery signal box, which opened in 1912 as Prince of Wales Sidings and was renamed from 21 November 1968.

On 30 December 1994, Prince of Wales was taken over by RJB Mining, and later by UK Coal in 2001. Despite spending £16 million to access new workings, UK Coal announced the mine's closure on 30 January 2002 as further investment could not be justified. Production ended on 30 August 2002, and the 500 workers were either offered redundancy or jobs at other collieries.

This was a difficult colliery in which to photograph trains, as their only exit was at the eastern end, controlled by Prince of Wales signal box. Therefore the only view of departing trains was obtained from the level crossing on Skinner Lane, unless access was gained to the colliery itself. One attempt to gain permission was met with refusal, so my only photograph was of 56055 departing the colliery on 2 September 1994. Despite the colliery remaining open for a further few years, I never returned.

Rossington

The Rossington Main Colliery Co. Ltd was a subsidiary of both the Sheepbridge Coal and Iron Co., who were working Cobnar Wood, Glapwell, and Langwith collieries in Derbyshire, and of John Brown and Co., who owned Aldwarke Main and Car House collieries near Rotherham. The chosen site was about 1.75 miles west of Rossington, close to the then LNER East Coast Main Line from where a branch line was laid.

Sinking the 22-foot-diameter No. 1 shaft began on 10 July 1912, but work stopped after two weeks due to an inrush of water. Work resumed on 21 February 1913, and the Barnsley seam was reached on 3 May 1915 at a depth of 872 yards. Sinking continued until the Dunsil seam was cut about 15 yards below. Work on the 22-foot-diameter No. 2 shaft commenced on 26 June 1912, which reached the Barnsley seam on 7 November 1915 and the Dunsil seam on 18 November.

Production from the Barnsley seam began in July 1916 and continued until final closure in 2006. The Dunsil seam was also worked at various times (1917–22, 1925–27, 1955–58, and 1983–91) throughout the colliery's life.

Rossington became part of Yorkshire Amalgamated Collieries Ltd in 1927, but continued trading under its own name until 1936, when it became Amalgamated Denaby Collieries Ltd until nationalisation.

Conveyors were used in the Barnsley seam from January 1933, and in 1939, Britain's first flame-proof diesel locomotive was used underground for moving men and coal. From 1952, methane extracted from strata near the faces was piped from the mine and pumped 10 miles to Manvers Main, where it fired coke ovens.

A modernisation project in 1963–5 saw the building of a 48-m (157-foot) high headgear on both shafts, with electrically-powered friction winders at ground level. Power-loading replaced hand-working in June 1964, and powered roof supports were used from September 1965.

The introduction of trunk conveyors and bunkerage began in 1969 to carry the coal from the face to the skips in the pit bottom, and a pad loading scheme for MGR trains opened on the surface in 1971.

In April 1993, Rossington was closed but put on care and maintenance while a buyer was sought. It was reopened by RJB Mining (UK) Ltd as a private mine in July 1994, with the colliery branch reopening on 15 December 1994. In 1996, Budge bought the mine, extending its operating license from ten to twenty-five years. In 2000, the mine passed to UK Coal Mining Ltd.

Unfortunately, the area of coal then being worked was found to be affected by faulting, with a severe consequence on output. The resultant losses, together with the cost of developing further resources, led to UK Coal closing Rossington, and production ended on Friday, 31 March 2000. The site was demolished in 2007, and after the tip was reworked and landscaped, it was designated for housing development.

It was only after seeing an image in *Rail* magazine that I gave thought to visit Rossington, despite the close proximity to my home. Consequently, only two visits were ever made within the timescale of this book, although further visits were made in the 2000s. On my first visit, I had missed the loading of the train, instead managing to photograph it departing from the run-round loop adjacent to the ECML. Permission from the manager was granted for my second visit, so I was allowed free reign to photograph the loading process, and then walk along the branch to photograph the train leaving the colliery. On subsequent occasions in the 2000s, I was even permitted to ride along the branch in the brake van.

The first time I visited Rossington, I missed the train I went for as it had already left and was in the run-round loop adjacent to the East Coast Main Line. It was thus a mad dash to find a spot to photograph it, and this is the result. Here, 56067 has already run around and is leaving Rossington loop with 7F78 Rossington to Grimethorpe Coalite on 17 December 1993.

On my second visit, the train had just arrived. Here with Rossington Colliery headstocks in the background, 58019 *Shirebrook Colliery* is being loaded to form 7G36 to West Burton on 7 February 1995. Notice the ground position light on its tall pole on the left.

A second view of 58019 *Shirebrook Colliery* as it is being loaded to form 7G36 to West Burton on 7 February 1995. The gantry over the line was used for checking the wagons were empty as they were propelled through, and the upturned mine cars are full of concrete, which were placed across the tracks after each train to prevent dirt bikers using the track as a race ground.

As the train was loaded, it was moved forward to allow the loading shovels to load more wagons. As viewed from the spoil heap, loading is almost complete, and it will not be long before the train is ready to depart.

No. 58019 *Shirebrook Colliery* is departing from the colliery and making its way towards the run-round loop adjacent to the ECML with 7G36 to West Burton on 7 February 1995.

On 17 February 1996, Hertfordshire Rail Tours ran 'the Friar Tuck' rail tour, which originated at Kings Cross and took in various lines that included the Rossington Colliery Branch. The train was top and tailed by 37718 *Hartlepool Pipe Mill* and 47540 *The Institution of Civil Engineers*. In this image, the 'Dutch'-liveried 47540 brings up the rear of the train as it arrives at Rossington Colliery.

No. 37718 *Hartlepool Pipe Mill n*ow brings up the rear as the rail tour makes its way around the curve of the colliery branch towards the run-round loop on 17 February 1996.

New Sharlston

Sharlston Colliery was sunk in an area that had seen coal mining since medieval times. It was situated 3.75 miles east of Wakefield, on the exposed West Riding coalfield and the edge of the village of New Sharlston.

The original workings were shallow and based on seams that outcropped in the area. These were the Sharlston Top seam, which was 40 inches thick at a depth of 58 yards, the 38-inch-thick Sharlston Low seam at 75 yards, and the 36-inch-thick Sharlston Yard seam at a depth of 104 yards. Over the course of time, new shafts were opened and the mine changed hands. The opening of the Wakefield, Pontefract, and Goole Railway in 1848, followed by the Great Northern Railway between Askern, Doncaster, and Kings Cross, opened Sharlston's coal to wider markets.

In 1858, Richard Pope leased 1,034 acres of the Sharlston Top and Low seams, followed by a further lease on 1,034 acres of the Sharlston Yard seam in 1860. Along with partner Edward Baines Jr, they began sinking two shafts to the Sharlston Yard seam, which was reached in October 1861. However, this coal was of low quality and so deeper seams were aimed for.

With the death of Baines Jr, his father, Baines Sr, took over his shareholding. In need of capital to expand the mine, John Crossley and Sons, Carpet Manufacturers of Halifax, and J. M. Kirk (a Halifax-based wool dyer) were approached as both companies used coal to power their works. As such, the four partners formed the Sharlston Coal Company Ltd in May 1865, and the sinking of two 13-foot-diameter shafts began in June 1865. The 37-inch-thick scale seam was found at a depth of 313 yards, followed by the 107-inch-thick Stanley Main seam at a depth of 331 yards in July 1867.

The Crossley Company purchased J. M. Kirk's shares in 1867, thus becoming the majority shareholder in the New Sharlston Colliery. Later seams worked were the Winter, Haigh Moor, and Silkstone seams, which, after exhaustion, were replaced by the Warren House, Barnsley, and Stanley Main seams. By 1946, the colliery was producing 6,637 tons of coal per week and, with nationalisation in 1947, became part of the NCB North Eastern Division No. 7 Wakefield Area Sub Area B. It was employing 1,180 men underground and 320 on the surface at that time, which increased to 1,800 men by 1953, producing 11,500 tons per week.

In 1968, a 1,200-ton-capacity rail rapid-loading bunker was commissioned at a cost of £375,000. The Haigh Moor upcast shaft winding headgear was replaced in 1983 with one brought from Prince of Wales pit to increase coal tonnage drawn to the surface. The downcast shaft was named the Birkwood shaft, where men and materials travelled.

In 1984, 1,000 miners were employed, but with the advent of the miners' strike, things would change. Despite the relentless pit closures elsewhere, the future of Sharlston seemed assured as the NCB had invested millions during the late 1980s and early 1990s opening new coal reserves. Unfortunately, due to the exhaustion of viable reserves, closure was announced in 1992. The final night shift was on 28 May 1993 and Sharlston closed forever despite almost 8 million tons of workable reserves remaining. Of the 535 miners employed, 150 transferred to the Selby coalfield with the remainder taking redundancy. The shafts were filled and capped, and both headgears were felled in late 1993.

My one and only visit to Sharlston was post-closure on 2 September 1994, to witness the first train to run in order to remove the massive stockpiles. Unusually for this kind of operation, the rapid-loading bunker was still in use. Having photographed the train being loaded, I went to the exit from the colliery branch to get a shot passing the level crossing over High Street. This was unusual as although it was train man operated, it had traditional crossing gates but also barriers as well, which no doubt would have usurped the gates had the colliery not closed. Only the gates were used that day.

As I had family in the area, taking time out to visit before returning again allowed me to get the second train of the day, 7F31 at 5.18 p.m., as it departed the colliery branch.

Above: Having never been to Sharlston before, it took a while to find the location, but I decided to make the effort for the first train to be loaded from the closed colliery stockpile. On 2 September 1994, 56118 is seen as it has almost finished loading 7F30 for Ferrybridge under the bunker; this was unusual as at most closed collieries, the bunker would be demolished along with the colliery.

Below: A second shot from the spoil heap shows that just a handful of wagons remain to be loaded of 7F30 for Ferrybridge.

Loading complete, 56118 is preparing to run round its train to make 7F30 for Ferrybridge on 2 September 1994.

While the train was running around, I made my way over to the trainman-operated level crossing on High Street; here the traditional crossing gates were closed, but as can be seen, the barriers that would have usurped the gates were still raised. No. 56118 now approaches the main line connection where it would be held to wait the passage of a train.

As it was held, this gave me time to change positions, and here is 56118 as it leaves the colliery branch and joins the Pontefract line, as viewed from old Sharlston station platform, which closed in 1958.

After depositing its coal at Ferrybridge, 56118 returned with the empties to work the second train of the day at 5.18 p.m. and is now seen leaving the colliery branch. This train was 7F31 Sharlston to Ferrybridge on 2 September 1994. The white building behind is the Station public house, now closed.

No. 56118 now joins the Pontefract line as it works the second train of the day, 7F31 on the 5.18 p.m. Sharlston to Ferrybridge on 2 September 1994.

Silverwood

Dalton Main Collieries Ltd became a public company floated on the London Stock Exchange in December 1899, its purpose being to buy out the business of Roundwood Colliery, purchase land between Thrybergh and Ravenfield on Hollings Lane, and sink a new deep mine. Silverwood Colliery was therefore sunk between April 1900 and December 1903. Originally named Dalton Main, it was renamed after local woodlands.

Two 21-foot-diameter shafts were sunk in April 1900, and coal was being worked from the Barnsley seam at a depth of 740 yards in December 1903. By 1912, the colliery was producing 27,000 tons per year from a workforce of 3,467 underground and 828 on the surface. The First World War took its toll on the workers, and by 1919, another 700 men were taken on to get the colliery back up to full production.

The year 1949 saw 3,000 men at the mine, and plans were being made to exploit the Meltonfield seam that, by the early 1950s, was producing low-quality coal. The Barnsley seam was becoming expensive to work, and so the Swallowood seam was opened up and began production in 1967, as did the Haigh Moor seam. The Barnsley seam was closed down in 1972, but by 1974, the colliery was producing 1 million tons per year from a workforce of 1,300. The years 1975–6 saw the construction of a 3,500-ton rapid-loading bunker at a cost of £1 million, in order to accommodate increasing demands for coal from the CEGB.

Further injections of money into the colliery in the 1980s brought the Swallowood and Haigh Moor seams up to full production, with most of the coal being sent to the power stations.

The 1990s were a decade of change for the pits and Silverwood was no different, although the colliery was sending out 14,000 tons per week to West Burton power station. Although plans were announced to develop the Parkgate seam, this never happened and the colliery closed in December 1994, with the remaining reserves being worked from nearby Maltby Main Colliery. Following demolition, large stockpiles remained, and a large coal-washing and reclamation project was set up, with trains collecting reclaimed coal and transporting it to the Aire Valley power stations.

As for the rail connection to the colliery, the railway companies serving the nearby Roundwood Colliery were approached to build a line to Silverwood but both declined and so it was built privately as 'the Roundwood and Dalton Colliery Railway'. The line was opened in 1901, and its main engineering work was a girder bridge crossing the River Don, which was built by Newton, Chambers and Company. The line was known for its gradients, the main section being between 1 in 44 and 1 in 56.

The line became part of the Rotherham, Maltby, and Laughton Railway, which, in turn, became the major part of the Great Central and Midland Railway's Joint Committee in South Yorkshire. The line commenced from the GCR Rotherham to Mexborough line at Thrybergh Junction and continued on from Silverwood via Ravenfield, to join the existing Brancliffe East Junction to Dinnington Colliery line just north of Anston. The line beyond Silverwood to Hellaby (Great Central, Hull & Barnsley and Midland Joint Railway) was closed in 1967 for the construction of a motorway bridge; it never reopened, being officially closed from March 1969.

Rationalisation of rail facilities commenced with the introduction of a rapid-loading bunker in 1975. The main line from Thrybergh Junction to Silverwood was singled, and after closure of the colliery, further reductions were made.

With the clearing out of stocks, a new method of working was introduced that required top and tailing trains. This is explained further in the captions.

My only visit to the colliery in its working capacity was on 15 December 1993 when I photographed both train and rapid-loader bunker. At my next visit, the stocks were being cleared out and the site was a sea of mud.

The bridge over the railway at Hollings Lane allowed a good view of the train, and here, 58034 awaits permission to enter the bunker on 15 December 1993.

Above left: My first visit to Silverwood Colliery while it was a working pit allowed for this view taken from the Hollings Lane overbridge between Dalton and Ravenfield. Here, 58034 Bassetlaw is moving towards the bunker ready for loading 6F88 for Cottam power station on 15 December 1993.

Above right: No. 58037 with 7G40 Silverwood Colliery to West Burton power station is seen leaving the Silverwood branch at Thrybergh Junction and taking the line towards Mexborough on 5 September 1994. The single line to its right goes to Roundwood Junction where it connects to the Swinton to Aldwarke Junction line.

To better describe the operations of the Silverwood branch, what better place to start than by showing a series of photos. Here, looking at the colliery branch during operations to remove coal stocks after closure. Nos 56082 and 56083 cross the Newton Chambers and Company 1901-built bridge over the River Don at the start of the Silverwood branch, with 6F71 from Milford to Silverwood. This image was taken during the last week of trains on 5 June 1996.

There were no run-round facilities at the colliery itself, these being at the former Silverwood Junction, which was where the line into the colliery connected to the branch from Thrybergh Junction. This line was originally to Braithwell but closed beyond Silverwood. This is the view of the connection from the Silverwood branch to the actual colliery and shows 6F72 Sudforth Lane to Silverwood as it arrives on 10 May 1996. No. 56083 has been detached from 56078 and is moving forward to the points; it will then move onto the colliery connection where it will wait until the other loco draws the train forward.

No. 56083 has now been reattached to the rear of the train and is pulling it onto the colliery line towards the loading area on 10 May 1996. No. 56078, now on the rear, will be detached from the train before it gets to the point and the train will then continue to the loading area with the lead engine only. Meanwhile, after the points are reversed, 56078 will then move onto the line back towards Thrybergh where it will wait until the train has loaded. On the horizon far right are the twin cooling towers of Blackburn Meadows power station that stood alongside the M1 motorway until demolition in August 2008.

On a freezing 19 February 1996, operations began to move the stocks, and on the following day, 20 February, I made the pilgrimage to get photos. Here, 56084 is seen as it is loading 7H19 for Eggborough power station. The second loco was out of view around the corner waiting for the train to be propelled back.

A closer view of 7H19 being loaded on 20 February 1996.

Opposite middle: No. 56027 waits on the single line for the loaded train to be propelled back from the colliery, the connection being on the right. It will then couple up and double head 7H19 from Silverwood to Drax as far as Hexthorpe in Doncaster on 20 February 1996. The high-level shots were taken from the spoil heap on the right.

Opposite below: The things we do for a photo—while waiting for the train to set back from the colliery, snow began to fall again, but it was Baltic conditions before 56027 coupled to 56084 and was ready to depart Silverwood, double-headed as far as Hexthorpe on 20 February 1996.

Once loaded, the train is propelled back from the loading area onto the Silverwood branch. Here, as viewed from Hollings Lane, 56074 *Kellingley Colliery* is propelling 7H06 Silverwood to Drax away from the colliery on 10 May 1996.

Woolley

Woolley Colliery was situated alongside the 1850-opened Barnsley to Wakefield line close to Darton station, 3.5 miles north-west of Barnsley. The main mine began as a pair of tunnels into the hillside in the Barnsley Bed seam, worked by two partners—Captain Marsden and Mr Armitage, who formed the Woolley Coal Company in 1853. Production at the new Woolley Colliery began the next year, and as time went on, vertical shafts were sunk to get at the deeper seams. The first shafts sunk at Woolley were at Wheatley Wood, which found the Beamshaw seam at a depth of 88 yards. Then at 220 yards, they found the Winter seam in 1869.

In 1894, ownership changed to Fountain and Burnley. Two new shafts were sunk on the site of the modern colliery in 1912, which plummeted to 423 yards to access the Parkgate, Thorncliffe, Silkstone, and Blocking seams, some of which were very thin. In 1942, No. 3 shaft was sunk to the 2-foot 3-inch-thick Lidgett seam at 130 yards.

When the mine was nationalised in 1947, 2,384 men produced 649,931 tons of coal. In 1951, Woolley Colliery merged with the nearby Woolley Edge Colliery, thus allowing the latter's coal to be treated by the former's washing plant. By 1967, manpower had decreased to 2,029, although output had increased to 841,625 tons. Two years later, 1,931 workers were turning out 1,019,553 tons following the installation of machinery and conveyor belts.

By 1970, coal was being produced from eight faces in four seams—the Lidgett, the Thorncliffe (3 feet 6 inches thick), the Silkstone (2 feet 7 inches thick), and the Blocking (2 feet 1 inch thick); further seams were being developed. At the end of the 1970s, 1,902 men were producing 870,000 tons from the top and low Haigh Moor, Thorncliffe, Parkgate, and Blocking seams. The markets for the coal were almost all industrial. Some 65 per cent of the output was utilised for the production of electricity, and 25 per cent went to the steel sector for coke making. Chemical works in Cheshire were also supplied.

Opened in August 1983, the new West Side coal preparation plant processed coal from several collieries, some of it travelling for miles underground. In June 1987, Redbrook Colliery was merged with Woolley, the latter becoming known as Woolley/Redbrook Colliery. This was a very short-lived merger as the whole colliery closed on 22 December 1987, with the loss of 1,100 jobs. The West Side CPP remained open to process coal from Denby Grange and Park Mill until the former's closure in July 1991. It was decommissioned but not demolished until 21 February 1993. The area was subsequently cleared and partially open-casted, but today, it is a housing estate.

My first trip there was towards the end of the 1990s, on 6 September 1999. After chatting for a while to the Woolley signalman, I obtained a series of photos of 56119 undergoing loading 7C31 Woolley to Eggborough. Accessing the site was via a road down the hillside, and on my second visit, as I drove down the hill, I was greeted by a massive hole for the open casting operation. Emerging from the centre, almost skyscraper-like, was a tall, thin, concrete object. At first, I was puzzled as to what it was, but then it dawned on me—this was one of the shafts. The material around it had been dug away, leaving the exposed shaft. It was most weird.

Another closed colliery sends out its stockpiled coal. Here is 56119 at Wooley as two mechanical shovels load 7C31 Woolley to Eggborough power station on 6 September 1999.

Stepping a bit further back allowed a view of the relay room at Wooley, which also includes a small signalling panel, which is worked as a signal box to reduce the section between Barnsley and Meadowhall. No. 56119 is still being loaded here.

A higher viewpoint of 56119 as 7C31 Woolley to Eggborough is loaded. Traffic on the M1 motorway can be seen in the distance.

The final view at Wooley. Settling tanks can be seen in the foreground, and in the distance, the M1 motorway can clearly be seen on 6 September 1999.

6
Leicestershire and Staffordshire Area Collieries

As I only visited one colliery in Leicestershire and one in Staffordshire, their coverage is combined together here, beginning with the so-called Leicestershire 'Super Pit' at Asfordby.

Asfordby (Leicestershire Area)

With the closure of the mines in west Leicestershire, the so-called 'Super Pit' at Asfordby opened with the expectation of providing miners with jobs well into the twenty-first century. The initial exploration had begun in November 1973, and work in preparation for construction started in October 1984. In August 1985, work commenced to sink two 1,500-foot-deep shafts. The chosen site was west of Melton Mowbray, right on the southern edge of the huge coalfield, beneath the Vale of Belvoir—a fact that would have huge repercussions for the life of the pit.

The cost of the project, which opened in April 1995, was around £400 million, but on 15 August 1997, water started pouring in from the overlying water-bearing strata, flooding a new coal face. Despite best efforts, it proved impossible to pump the water clear, so the ventilation was cut off and the face closed down. After assessing the conditions of the mine, it was decided, after just two years of production, that it was too costly to continue, and the mine closed on 18 August 1997.

Rail access to the colliery was complex. Asfordby Colliery was situated alongside the long-closed former Midland Railway (MR) Holywell branch, formerly serving Holywell Iron Works and connected to the former Great Northern and London and North Western (GN&LNW) Joint Line to Newark. This branch connected to the former Nottingham–Melton Mowbray MR line (by then the Old Dalby test track). The branch connection was west–north, but when the colliery was opened, a new

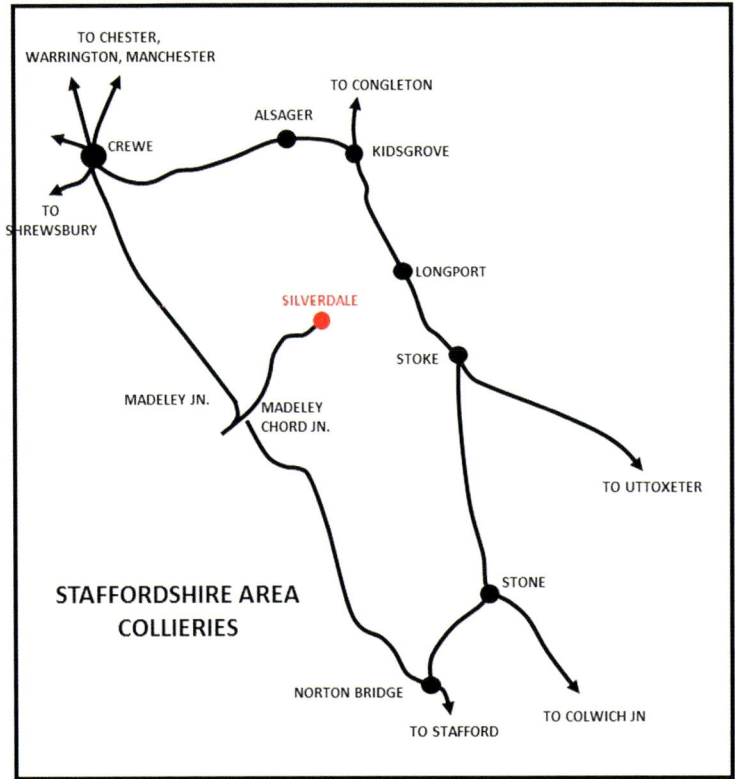

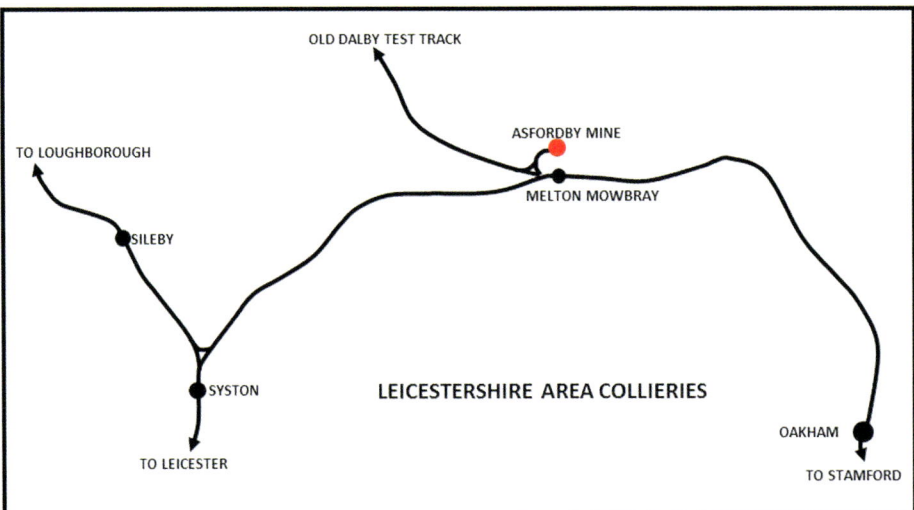

Map showing the location of Leicestershire and Staffordshire collieries. The coloured dots are locations photographed.

east-to-north curve was provided. In turn, the former Nottingham branch joined the MR Leicester–Peterborough line via an east-facing connection at Melton Junction, a short distance west of Melton Mowbray station.

Trains for Asfordby originated at Toton and were initially destined for Ratcliffe. For a train to access the colliery, it travelled from Toton via Syston Junction to Melton Mowbray, with a reversal here to access the Old Dalby track and the branch to the colliery. After loading, trains would again reverse at Melton Mowbray. Despite run-round facilities being provided at the colliery, all trains were top-and-tailed in order to save time.

Eight Class 58s—nos 58001, 003–005, 009, 010, 013, and 046—were modified with spring-loaded drawgear cannibalised from Class 47s, for specific use on the Asfordby traffic owing to sharp curvature. During the short production period, trains were pad-loaded at first until the rapid-loading bunker was completed. I only ever visited Asfordby once as the location was initially difficult to find. I subsequently purchased an ordnance survey map, which showed the location of the footbridge across the line near to the mine.

On 14 May 1996, with 58004 leading and 58003 *Markham Colliery* out of sight at the rear of the train, 6F70 from Toton approaches Asfordby as viewed from a footbridge that crosses the line close to the rail complex throat.

With 58004 now beyond the bunker, 58003 *Markham Colliery* brings up the rear. Once loaded, the train will form 7D69 for Ratcliffe. This was the only train I ever photographed at this location while it was a colliery. However, after closure, the site became a testing facility connected to the Old Dalby test track. Initially being used to commission Virgin Trains' new 'Pendolino' units, I did then return again to photograph the location.

A second view of 58003 *Markham Colliery* on the rear of 6F70.

With the demolished remains of Holywell Iron Works in the foreground, Mainline grey-liveried 58003 *Markham Colliery* takes the loaded 7D69 for Ratcliffe back towards Melton Mowbray, where it will reverse direction and head initially for Toton.

No. 58003 *Markham Colliery* and its train have now joined the Syston Junction to Peterborough line heading towards Melton Mowbray. Having passed beneath Leicester Road bridge, it is about to pass milepost 105 ¾, the mileage being taken from St Pancras. The train will continue another 0.25 miles or so to Melton Mowbray station, where it will enter the loop to reverse direction and then head back past the camera to Toton.

No. 58004 brings up the rear of the train as it heads towards the Melton Mowbray station loop. This image was taken from a public footpath between Tamar Road and Victor Avenue in Melton Mowbray.

Silverdale (Staffordshire Area)

By the time I made my first foray to the Staffordshire area, the coalfield, which covered an area of 70 sq. miles, had dwindled to just the one pit at Silverdale. Although it had its origins back in 1830, a new mine was built on the site in 1950 by the NCB. The colliery was completely rebuilt during the 1970s, when three new drifts were sunk to exploit new reserves in the Keele area.

Production increased, and over 1 million tons was mined annually. Despite that, British Coal decided to close the colliery and, under their ownership, the last coal was drawn in December 1993. That was not the end, however, as following privatisation in 1994, Silverdale was owned by Coal Investments and production re-commenced later that year. With the bankruptcy of Coal Investments, it was taken over by Midlands Mining in 1996.

Silverdale station sat on the Stoke to Market Drayton line; opened by the North Staffordshire Railway in May 1863, and closed in 1964. The station buildings remained for a number of years as train crew accommodation for rail staff who worked the coal trains to Silverdale Colliery, as the rapid-loader bunker was constructed adjacent to the former station. With the closure of the through route, the rail access to the colliery was from a 1962-built chord to provide a connection to the West Coast Main Line at Madeley Junction.

The subsequent layout therefore enforced another complex manoeuvre to access the colliery. The chord at Madeley Junction was made into the Down Slow and faced north, while the branch crossed the WCML at right angles. Trains arrived from the Crewe direction from the north, then crossed over to the chord in order to access the branch. The loco was required to run round its train before continuing to Silverdale. After loading beneath the rapid-loading bunker, the loco ran around and the train returned to the chord, for the third run round before re-joining the WCML.

The output from the colliery was latterly sent to Ironbridge and Fiddlers Ferry power stations, and as far away as West Burton, among others. Yet the end came in December 1998, and the last train to be loaded from the last deep mine in North Staffordshire was hauled away by 60037. Today, the closed and lifted branch forms part of a railway footpath to Newcastle-under-Lyme. Only the restored platforms remain—the station building was rebuilt at Apedale Heritage Centre.

I only ever visited the bridge adjacent to the rapid-loading bunker once, but obtained shots of the train in the run-round loop at Madeley. It was a long way from home, but the effort was worthwhile.

As viewed from a footbridge at the end of Station Road, 60100 *Boar of Badenoch* is loading 7Z66 Silverdale to Toton on 7 July 1998. Silverdale station building was to the right of the bunker, and this was a long way to go for a photo, but worth it.

After loading, 60100 trundles along the branch as viewed from Manor Road and is heading into the run-round loop at Madeley with 7Z66 Silverdale to Toton on 7 July 1998. *En route*, the line crosses the M6 motorway and the West Coast Main Line at right angles, with the train passing over the latter.

When the North Staffordshire Railway Stoke to Market Drayton Line was opened, a station called Madeley was opened. Within a few months, possibly to avoid confusion with the LNWR station that was, at least, on the edge of Madeley; the station was renamed Madeley Manor after the nearby abandoned house of that name. By August 18/1, the name had been changed yet again to Madeley Road. This is the site of the station, a train crew building having been erected on the site. No. 60100 has been detached from the train and is now running to the other end of the run-round loop.

Now at the far end of the run round, the driver has reset the points and is ready to run around the train. The line continued just around the corner but originally went as far as Market Drayton.

No. 60100 round past its train and will couple to the far end of the rake of HAAs to re-attach. It will then take the train down to join the WCML and head off to Toton.

7

Power Stations

Power Generation Privatisation

In 1990, the Central Electricity Generating Board (CEGB) was privatised and divided into four divisions (which ultimately became successor companies)—namely National Power, PowerGen, Nuclear Electric, and the National Grid Company. National Power and PowerGen between them shared England and Wales' coal-fired power stations, Nuclear Electric took over the nuclear power stations, and the National Grid was awarded control of the national electricity distribution system.

Of the power stations to feature in this book, PowerGen acquired High Marnham, Cottam, Ratcliffe, and Castle Donington. Meanwhile, National Power took over West Burton, Willington, Thorpe Marsh, Didcot, Eggborough, and Drax.

Trainload Coal worked closely with the electricity producers and signed new four-year contracts with them on 1 April 1990, giving a combined annual commitment to purchase 70 million tons of coal. This requirement was reduced to 65 million tons in 1993–4, with possible new coal sources coming on-stream as the UK collieries were closed and the existing contract with British Coal expired. Of course, this was imported coal, and to streamline its movement from Immingham to Cottam power station, a new curve was planned at Clarborough Junction. Here, the Cottam branch (on the former direct line to Lincoln via Torksey) diverges from the Retford to Gainsborough line.

The junction was east-facing so trains from Immingham via Lincoln or Brigg had to pass Clarborough (and hence Cottam) *en route* to Worksop to run around before returning to Clarborough to access the branch to Cottam. To cut down on mileage, a curve was planned to directly access the branch from the Gainsborough direction. Although the route was surveyed and pegged out, the plan was never proceeded with.

In the financial year ending 31 March 1991, Trainload Coal moved 73.8 million tons, of which 59.6 million tons was intended for the power stations. The coal sector was responsible for 60 per cent of the entire Trainload business.

This chapter will introduce each power station with a brief description, together with the trains I photographed in their environs. In the 1990s, I focused primarily on the coal traffic within the collieries and *en route* to the power stations, hence my collection of power station photos is much thinner. I managed to capture trains at those that were in the throes of closure, such as Willington, Castle Donnington, and Thorpe Marsh, while I only ever photographed one train at both Didcot and Staythorpe. High Marnham was a favourite location before that too succumbed to closure. I also photographed Ratcliffe-on-Soar, Cottam, and West Burton, of which only the latter was still active at the time of writing.

As a serving railwayman during British Rail days, I was fortunate in some respects in that I had the opportunity to ride in the cabs of trains serving the local power stations at West Burton, Cottam, and High Marnham.

Above: No. 58019 *Shirebrook Colliery* crosses Manton viaduct with another load of coal for West Burton power station as 7G42 from Clipstone on 21 December 1993.

Below: Mainline blue-liveried 58023 *Peterborough Depot* passes Brancliffe East Junction's signals with 7F87 Oxcroft Opencast to Cottam power station on 10 September 1997. This box closed in November 1997, its functions being taken over by Worksop PSB.

```
MGR WORKING TO POWER STATIONS(NAT.POWER)   WEEK COMM.SUNDAY 05.12.93
========================================   ==========================
WEST BURTON
-----------
HARWORTH       7,800   G30 0514 WFO    G54 1814 THSX
                       G40 0814 SO

KIVETON PARK  11,200   G36 0856 SX     G40 1056 MO
                       G42 1156 TTHO   G36 0800 SO
                       G44 1250 SO

MANTON         7,800   G50 1655 SUN    G70 0500 TTHO
                       G42 1300 WFO    G46 1600 TO
                       G38 0400 SO

SILVERWOOD    11,200   G64 2334 SUN    G68 0134 MO
                       G50 1534 TSX    G66 0040 MSX

GOLDTHORPE    12,300   G44 1006 SX     G58 1806 SX
                       G66 2306 FO

WARDLEY        1,100   G30 0406 SO                      EX MILFORD
               ------
TOTAL         51,400

NATIONAL POWER FLOWS SOUTH FROM THIS AREA
-----------------------------------------
RUGELEY
-------
.NONE FROM NORTHERN SECTION OF EAST MIDLANDS FREIGHT AREA

DIDCOT
------
WELBECK        7,800   V65 0720 EWD                     DIRECT TRAFFIC

BILSTHORPE     8,900   V32 0428 MO     V31 2256 SUN/SX  VIA TOTON
                       V30 1856 SUN
THORESBY      13,400   V49 0236 EWD    V32 0436 MX      VIA TOTON

BOLSOVER COALITE
----------------
KIVETON PARK   5,400   T27 1600 FSX    T27 0956 SO

NATIONAL POWER FLOWS NORTH FROM THIS AREA
-----------------------------------------
EGGBOROUGH
----------
HARWORTH      12,300   C02 0012 FO     C06 0900 SX
                       C09 1600 SX

A.M.BAVA
FOR AREA MANAGER, EAST MIDLANDS FREIGHT, NOTTINGHAM
```

MGR working to National Power-owned power stations for week commencing 5 December 1993. (*Courtesy James Skoyles*)

```
MGR WORKING TO POWER STATIONS( POWERGEN )-WEEK COMM.SUNDAY 05.12.93
========================================   ==========================
ALL TRAINS WILL COMPRISE 36 X 26/32 TONNE AIR BRAKED COAL HOPPERS,
UNLESS OTHERWISE SHOWN,AND THIS CIRCULAR IS THE AUTHORITY,TO CONVEY
THE STATED NUMBER OF LOADED WAGONS OVER ROUTES SHOWN.

LOADED TRAINS TO RUN CLASS 7, EMPTY TRAINS TO RUN CLASS 6.

COLLIERY         TONNAGE  SUMMARY OF SERVICES              STAGING POINT

COTTAM
-------
BILSTHORPE       13,000   F67 0133 MO      F41 1008 MTO
                          F59 2053 SX      F69 0243 MSX

HARWORTH         20,200   F65 0033 MO      F69 0253 MSO
                          F35 0550 MTTHO   F43 1118 SX
                          F49 1350 SX      F41 1018 SO
                          F47 1303 SO

MANTON           21,000   F57 2010 SUN     F61 2305 SUN
                          F39 1005 EWD     F55 1910 SX
                          F63 0015 MX      F33 0700 SO
                          F49 1350 SO

OLLERTON         20,200   F59 2050 SUN     F31 0506 EWD
                          F45 1306 SX      F61 2216 SX
                          F45 1200 SO

RAVENSTRUTHER    13,200   Y56 0610 WFSO    Y58 0715 MX    EX MILFORD
                          Y57 1515 MSX

WESTFIELD         6,600   Y57 1515 MO      Y59 2335 SX    EX MILFORD

WELBECK           5,500   F53 1727 SX
                         -------
       TOTAL    100,700

HIGH MARNHAM
------------
OLLERTON          5,500   H31 0739 MSX     H32 0954  MO

FERRYBRIDGE
-----------
HARWORTH          3,300   F31 0012 TWTHO

.****************************************************************
                            THE END.
.****************************************************************

T.C.KIRKHAM
FOR AREA MANAGER, EAST MIDLANDS FREIGHT, NOTTINGHAM.
```

MGR working to Powergen-owned power stations week commencing 5 December 1993. (*Courtesy James Skoyles*)

Castle Donington

This coal-fired power station was situated on the River Trent near Castle Donington in Leicestershire, 5 miles south-east of Derby. Construction began in 1951, and the station (with its six 100-MW turbo-generators) opened in 1958. Following privatisation in 1990, the station was operated by PowerGen. In 1993, four of the generating units were decommissioned, and in 1994, the remaining two units were taken out of operation and the station closed down.

After closure, the remaining coal stocks were removed by rail to nearby Ratcliffe power station. I only visited once, on 11 November 1993, and my photos were taken amid strange circumstances. Access to the power station was over a small level crossing at Back Lane, where a security hut and gates defended the power station land. Standing next to the security hut was a police constable, chatting to the security guard inside. When a friend and I arrived, we stood on the crossing to take the photos looking in to the power station. Although the PC looked but never uttered a word, the security guard gave us the look of death.

With the first photo taken, the security guard challenged us, but still the PC remained silent. We moved further up the road and photographed operations through the fence, at which point the security guard ran up the other side of the fence and stood in front of us, remonstrating with us for taking photos. Again we moved, and again he stood in front of us. We confused the guard by splitting up—my friend to the right and me to the left—and continued taking photos. With the mission accomplished, we walked back to the level crossing with the guard in pursuit, muttering continuously. We had expected to be reprimanded by the PC but he just looked at the guard, turned to us, shook his head, and carried on his conversation—very strange indeed.

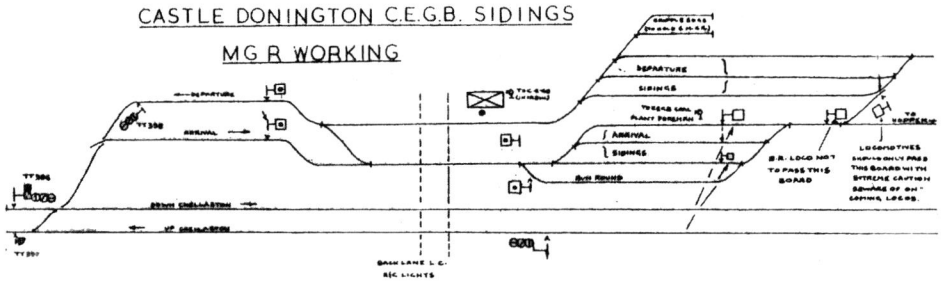

Castle Donington MGR working diagram dated 1981.

Andrew Barclay 0-4-0 shunters, Powergen Nos 1 and 2 are seen at Castle Donnington on 11 November 1993. It was at this point that the security guard mentioned came out of his cabin just off the photo and challenged me.

No. 58041 *Ratcliffe Power Station with* 7T63 for Ratcliffe via Toton leaves Castle Donnington power station as the removal of the stockpile begins. Andrew Barclay Locos Powergen Nos 1 and 2 are being passed as the train moves towards the exit gates.

Above left: As viewed from Station Road overbridge, 58034 *Bassetlaw* is seen as it arrives in the reception sidings at Castle Donnington to collect the next rake of loaded HAAs as 58041 departs with 7T63 for Ratcliffe on 11 November 1993.

Above right: Again as viewed from Station Road overbridge, 58041 now departs Castle Donnington with 7T63 for Ratcliffe on 11 November 1993.

Back at the power station, 58034 *Bassetlaw* has just arrived to take out the next rake of wagons on 11 November 1993. The power station has since been demolished and a distribution centre for Marks and Spencer has been developed on the site.

Cottam

Work started on the construction of the 2,000-MW Cottam power station in April 1964, on the site of Mickleholme Farm, near Retford. The architects were Yorke Rosenberg Mardall, and the main contractor was Balfour Beatty. The coal plant was supplied by the New Conveyor Company of Smethwick. John Thompson boilers supplied steam to English Electric 500-MW steam turbines, and the power station was opened in 1969.

Assuming a 100 per cent load factor, the station could consume 18,300 tons of coal per day, equating to 5 million tons per year. The maximum daily intake was 25,000 tons, brought in by rail originally from the East Midlands Coalfields, but latterly imported.

Access to the power station was via the then-disused Clarborough Junction to Sykes Junction line, which was truncated close to the site of Cottam station. A new formation was built towards the power station site, with a continuous loop formed for discharge. Under the control of automatic lineside equipment, trains moved forward at 0.5 mph, and the wagons unloaded their contents into a 600-ton-capacity underground hopper. The entire train could be unloaded in less than sixty minutes. From the underground hopper, the coal was either moved to the 9,200-ton-capacity bunkers in the boiler house or to the coal-stocking area.

The central control room, situated adjacent to the unloading hopper, controlled all of the coal plant operations, including the signalling within the power station loop.

Table 7 shows the coal plan for week ending 24 June 1995, which provides an idea of the number of trains serving the power station at the time. Despite being local to Cottam, I was very remiss about photographing there, and therefore have very few images from the timescale covered.

Table 7: Cottam Power Station Train List (Week Ending 24 June 1995)					
Train ID	Depart Colliery	Days Run	Colliery Origin	Power Station Arrive/Depart	
7F01	21.19	MWFO	Rufford	00.45	01.55
7F02	18.14	SX	Harworth	01.55	03.05
7F03	23.30	SUN	Welbeck	03.05	04.15
7F03	00.39	TO	Rufford	03.05	04.15
7F04	20.50	TThO	Welbeck	03.05	04.15
7F03	00.39	ThSO	Rufford	03.05	04.15
7F05	03.14	MSX	Harworth	06.25	07.35
7F05	03.59	SO	Rufford	06.25	07.35
7F06	04.50	TThO	Welbeck	07.30	08.40
7F06	06.40	SO	Harworth	08.30	09.40
7F07	09.05	FSX	Manton	09.35	10.45
7F07	09.05	FO	Manton	09.35	10.45
7F07	09.05	SO	Manton	09.35	10.45
7F08	07.20	MWFO	Ollerton	10.35	11.45

7F08	07.20	TThO	Ollerton	10.35	11.45
7F08	08.09	SO	Bilsthorpe	10.35	11.45
7F09	09.14	MO	Rufford	11.40	12.50
7F09	09.14	SO	Rufford	11.40	12.50
7F10	09.30	MTWO	Oxcroft	12.40	13.50
7F09	08.40	FO	Bilsthorpe	12.40	13.50
7F10	09.52	SO	Oxcroft	12.40	13.50
7F11	11.47	SO	Oxcroft	14.25	15.35
7F11	13.55	SX	Manton	14.25	15.35
7F12	12.50	SO	Welbeck	15.30	16.40
7F12	13.53	MO	Welbeck	15.30	16.40
7F12	14.04	TThO	Rufford	15.30	16.40
7F12	13.53	WFO	Welbeck	15.30	16.40
7F13	17.05	MO	Manton	17.35	18.40
7F13	12.25	TThO	Ollerton	17.35	18.40
7F13	12.25	FO	Ollerton	17.35	18.40
7F14	15.15	TO	Oxcroft	18.35	19.45
7F14	15.30	ThO	Welbeck	18.35	19.45
7F14	17.06	MWO	POW	19.40	20.50
7F14	17.27	FO	Ollerton	19.40	20.50
7F15	18.14	TThO	Rufford	20.10	21.50
7F15	19.31	SUN	Maltby	22.25	23.35
7F16	20.40	SUN	Welbeck	23.35	00.45
7F16	13.14	MWFO	Harworth	23.35	00.45
7F16	17.27	TThO	Ollerton	23.35	00.45
POW= Prince of Wales					

On 7 January 2019, EDF Energy announced that Cottam was due to cease generation on 30 September 2019 after more than fifty years of operation, and on Wednesday, 19 June 2019, GBRf delivered the last coal service to Cottam. The train, which consisted of a full rake of wagons but with just two loaded wagons containing 140 tonnes of coal, was hauled by 66735 and ran as 6F81 from Doncaster Decoy to Cottam, departing empty as 4D82 on the 12 p.m. Cottam to Doncaster Down Decoy. There was a Network Rail ultrasonic test train move to the power station on 11 September, and by 21 September, there was just 500 tons of coal remaining on the stockpile. This was burnt over the next two days, and the last day for generating power was to be on Monday 23 September; this was to be unit 1, which was the first unit to generate power and, in the end, the last. The very last train to use the power station branch was the UK Railtours 'Cottam Farewell' on Saturday, 28 September 2019. By the time this book is published, demolition will most likely be underway, or possibly even completed.

```
.COTTAM POWER STATION - OCCUPATION -        WEEK COMM.SUNDAY 05.12.93.
.===================================        =========================

TRIP REP.  DEP.  DAYS                       ARR.  DEP.  EMPTIES
NMBR NMBR  TIME  RUN    FROM                TIME  TIME  TO
---- ----  ----  -----  --------------------  ----  ----  ----------------
***************************************************************************
*SUNDAY/MONDAY 5TH & 6TH DECEMBER 1993                                   *
*----------------------------------------                                *
 T01  7F57  2010  SUN    MANTON              2040  2150  WORKSOP         *
 T02  7F59  2050  SUN    OLLERTON            2225  2335  WORKSOP         *
 T03  7F61  2305  SUN    MANTON              2335  0045  WORKSOP         *
 T04  7F65  0033  MO     HARWORTH            0155  0305  WORKSOP         *
 T01  7F67  0133  MO     BILSTHOPRE          0305  0415  WORKSOP         *
 T02  7F69  0253  MO     HARWORTH            0415  0525  WORKSOP         *
***************************************************************************
 T01  7F31  0506  SX     OLLERTON            0625  0735  WORKSOP         *
 T02  6Y56  0610  WFO    RAVENS X MILFORD    0830  0940  MILFORD  6R74   *
 T02  7F35  0550  MTTHO  HARWORTH            0830  0940  WORKSOP         *
 T04  6Y58  0715  MSX    RAVENS X MILFORD    0935  1045  MILFORD  6R78   *
 T03  7F39  1005  SX     MANTON              1035  1145  WORKSOP         *
 T05  7F41  1008  MTO    BILSTHORPE          1140  1250  WORKSOP         *
 T01  7F43  1118  SX     HARWORTH            1240  1350  WORKSOP         *
 T02  7F45  1306  SX     OLLERTON            1425  1535  WORKSOP         *
 T03  7F49  1350  SX     HARWORTH            1630  1740  WORKSOP         *
 T04  6Y57  1515  MO     WESTFIELD X MILFORD 1735  1845  MILFORD  6R76   *
 T04  6Y57  1515  MSX    RAVENS X MILFORD    1735  1845  MILFORD  6R76   *
 T05  7F53  1727  SX     WELBECK             1835  1945  WORKSOP         *
 T01  7F55  1910  SX     MANTON              1940  2050  WORKSOP         *
 T02  7F59  2053  SX     BILSTHORPE          2225  2335  WORKSOP         *
 T03  7F61  2216  SX     OLLERTON            2335  0045  WORKSOP         *
 T14  7F63  0015  MX     MANTON              0045  0155  WORKSOP         *
 T04  6Y59  2335  SX     WESTFIELD X MILFORD 0155  0305  MILFORD  6R77   *
 T05  7F69  0243  MSX    BILSTHORPE          0415  0525  WORKSOP         *
 T05  7F69  0253  SO     HARWORTH            0415  0525  WORKSOP         *
***************************************************************************
SATURDAY 11TH DECEMBER 1993                                              *
===========================                                              *
 T01  7F31  0506  SO     OLLERTON            0625  0735  WORKSOP         *
 T02  7F33  0700  SO     MANTON              0730  0840  WORKSOP         *
 T03  6Y56  0610  SO     RAVENS X MILFORD    0830  0940  MILFORD  6R74   *
 T04  6Y58  0715  SO     RAVENS X MILFORD    0935  1045  MILFORD  6R78   *
 T05  7F39  1005  SO     MANTON              1035  1145  WORKSOP         *
 T01  7F41  1018  SO     HARWORTH            1140  1250  WORKSOP         *
 T02  7F45  1200  SO     OLLERTON            1425  1535  WORKSOP         *
 T10  7F47  1303  SO     HARWORTH            1530  1640  WORKSOP         *
 T05  7F44  1350  SO     MANTON              1630  1740  WORKSOP         *
***************************************************************************
```

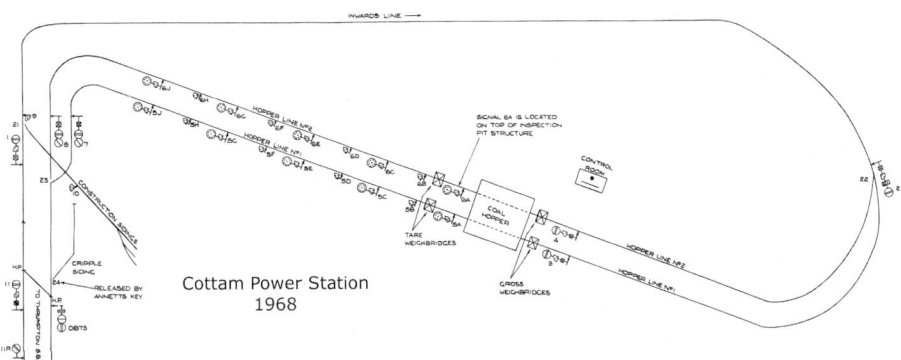

Diagram of signalling of the Cottam power station loop as issued to drivers.

Above left: Cottam power station from the air. The rail connection can be seen coming in on the right towards the bottom, heading towards the power station and then turning left for the loop just after the road bridge. The line of trees in the bottom right quarter is the original route onwards to Sykes Junction on the Gainsborough to Lincoln line.

Above right: As viewed from the road overbridge, 56021 is arriving with 7F41 Manton Colliery to Cottam on 5 May 1993.

After discharging its load, 58029 *Rugeley Power Station* is now departing Cottam with 6F04 to Worksop on 2 June 1994.

No. 58046 *Thoresby Colliery* on Hopper Line No. 1, moves slowly towards the discharge bunker at Cottam power station in May 1995.

No. 58046 is now entering the discharge bunker shed on Hopper Linc No. 1. The signal is No. 3, which is controlled from the main coal plant control room.

The main coal plant control room at Cottam complete with replica Cottam power station nameplate as attached to 58040. This is where all the coal operations are managed, including the signalling for the power station loop. With the closure of the power station in September 2019, the nameplate has been given to a coal plant employee.

The remaining 500 tonnes of coal waits to be removed from the once huge stockpile at Cottam power station on 21 September 2019. (*Author's collection*)

Didcot

The £104 million, 2,000-MW Didcot 'A' coal-fired power station was designed by architect Frederick Gibberd. Construction began during 1964 and was completed in 1968. The main chimney was 650 feet tall, with the six cooling towers each 375 feet high.

Didcot was served by a loop from the Great Western Main Line west of Didcot Parkway station. Initially, the coal was provided from the Nottinghamshire coalfields, but imported coal from Immingham was also supplied. Worksop-based drivers worked the Immingham trains as far as Toton. When the Midlands mines were closed, the coal was latterly supplied from South Wales or Avonmouth.

Didcot 'A' opted out of the large combustion plant directive, which meant it was only allowed to run for up to 20,000 hours after 1 January 2008 and had to close by 31 December 2015 at the latest. The decision was taken not to install flue gas desulphurisation equipment, which would have allowed continued generation, and as such, the station ceased operation at 2 p.m. on 22 March 2013.

The final train of imported coal arrived at 6.35 p.m. on 19 March 2013 as 6D17 Avonmouth to Didcot, hauled by 66117 and, after unloading the train, departed at 8.48 p.m. as 4D18 to Avonmouth.

Demolition of the power station started the following year, with the three southern cooling towers demolished by explosives on Sunday, 27 July 2014, at 5.01 a.m. Sadly, during demolition, four workers lost their lives due to a collapse of the boiler house.

I had visited Didcot many times but mostly to photograph from Parkway station. On one occasion in the 1990s, I decided to walk to the power station to photograph a train. Walking via Foxhall Road and Basil Hill Road to the overbridge on Milton Road must have seemed like a good idea at the time as the weather was dull with heavy cloud at the station but had started to snow heavily by then. Undaunted, I awaited the arrival of the train from Avonmouth and obtained its photo. I moved position and waited in the snow for the train's departure—sometimes, I do suffer for my art.

Table 8 shows a typical train list in week commencing 14 April 1991, and although I returned to Didcot again, the photos taken in 2006 are outside the scope of this book.

Table 8: Didcot Power Station Train List (Week Commencing 14 April 1991)						
Train ID	Depart Colliery	Days Run	Colliery Origin	Power Station Arrive/Depart		Train Recess/ Next working
Barrow Hill						
T04	08.55	SX	Oxcroft	09.10	1015	Light Diesel
T14	12.40	SX	Oxcroft	12.55	14.00	Light Diesel
N09	19.46	SUN	Markham	20.00	21.30	Markham
N11	23.11	SUN	Markham	03.27	23.42	Light Diesel
N13	03.17	MO	Markham	03.33	05.44	Markham
N14	07.25	MO	Markham	07.41	07.56	Light Diesel

N13	03.17	MX	Markham	03.33	05.44	Markham
N14	07.25	MX	Markham	07.41	07.56	Light Diesel
N24	16.34	SX	Markham	16.50	17.55	Light Diesel
Didcot						
Y30	21.34	SUN	Barrow Hill	02.28	04.00	Barrow Hill
Y31	00.01	MO	Barrow Hill	05.06	06.46	Barrow Hill
Y31	00.06	MSX	Barrow Hill	05.06	06.46	Barrow Hill
Y31	00.30	SO	Barrow Hill	05.06	06.46	Barrow Hill
Y32	03.26	TWFO	Barrow Hill	08.35	11.04	Barrow Hill
Y32	03.35	SO	Barrow Hill	08.35	11.04	Barrow Hill
Y49	05.20	EWD	Barrow Hill	10.34	12.32	Barrow Hill
Y85	13.00	SX	Barrow Hill	18.37	20.05	Barrow Hill
Y30	21.35	SO	Barrow Hill	02.28	04.00	Barrow Hill
Washwood Heath						
N43	14.51	SO	Barrow Hill	17.45		
Y03	04.48	SUN	Washwood Heath	19.27	21.00	Barrow Hill
Shirebrook Sidings						
N65	03.37	TThO	Welbeck	03.52	05.07	Light Diesel
Didcot						
Z65	10.00	TThO	Shirebrook Sdgs	14.36	16.37	Warsop
Z64	06.38	MX	Welbeck	11.37	13.40	Warsop
Z68	14.38	SX	Welbeck	20.15	21.50	Warsop
Toton						
Z30	16.15	MThO	Dixons	17.06	18.49	Dixons

No. 60010 *Pumlumon/Plynlimon* comes off the main line connection and heads for Didcot power station with 6A65 from Avonmouth on a particularly dreary 7 December 1995. The Great Western Main Line can be seen behind.

After discharging its load 60010 *Pumlumon/Plynlimon* now departs from Didcot with 6C65 to Avonmouth, where the set will again be loaded.

Before it can head westwards to Bristol, 60010 *Pumlumon/Plynlimon* prepares to run around its train at Didcot to return to Avonmouth on 7 December 1995.

Drax

The 3,870-MW Drax power station has the highest generating capacity of any UK power station, providing around 6 per cent of the country's electricity supply. At the time of its construction, it was also the largest coal-fired power station in Europe. Drax was constructed and commissioned in two stages—stage one (units 1, 2, and 3) was completed in 1974, and stage two (units 4, 5, and 6) was completed twelve years later in 1986.

The rail access to the power station is equally of interest as it was formed from parts of two disused railways—the NER Selby to Goole line, and the Hull and Barnsley Railway's (H&BR) Doncaster to Hull line. The H&BR line crossed the NER Knottingley to Goole line near Hensall, with a connection between the two being constructed later. The H&BR then passed beneath the NER Selby to Goole line close to Camblesforth. The planning and construction of Drax envisaged the incoming rail-borne coal originating from the Selby coalfield. Part of the H&BR line was reopened for 4 miles, diverging from a reinstated junction at Hensall. Originally known as Hensall Junction, it was renamed 'Drax Power Station Branch Junction', but was later shortened to Drax Branch Junction. At the point where the H&BR line passed beneath the Selby to Goole line near Camblesforth, a new connection was laid to join the two, and a section of the NER line was re-laid to take trains to the power station loop line.

The original loop was single-track with three coal-unloading lines. The loop was later doubled to cater for traffic bringing in limestone and taking gypsum out for the desulphurisation process. Further expansion in 2013 saw a new double-track unloading facility for the new biomass traffic.

During the mid-1990s, Drax could receive up to thirty trains per day. While the majority of those originated from the Selby complex at Gascoigne Wood, other regular sources included Prince of Wales, Widdrington, Wardley, Butterwell, Rossington, Welbeck, and Thoresby. Additionally, coal also originated from Markham Main, Maltby, Harworth, and Kellingley, together with imports from Immingham. Table 9 shows a typical week's coal plan in late 1993.

Table 9: Typical Week of Drax Arrivals, Late 1993		
Origin	Arrive	Days
Selby	00.36	SX + SuO
Thoresby	01.36	SX
Selby	02.06	EWD
Selby	02.51	SuO
Selby	03.36	EWD
Selby	04.01	SuO
Selby	04.16	MX
Blindwells	04.56	MX
Selby	05.11	SuO
Selby	05.36	EWD

Thoresby	06.11	WThFO
Selby	06.16	SuO
Selby	06.36	MX
Selby	07.06	EWD
Selby	07.36	SuO
Welbeck	08.06	MX
Selby	08.36	MO+SuO
Selby	09.06	EWD
Selby	09.31	SuO
Selby	10.26	EWD
Selby	10.51	SuO
Welbeck	11.06	MX
Selby	12.06	EWD
Selby	12.11	SuO
Thoresby	12.36	SX
Selby	13.36	SX
Selby	14.06	SuO
Selby	14.36	SX
Selby	15.36	SuO
Selby	15.40	SX
Selby	16.06	SO
Selby	16.36	SuO
Thoresby	16.38	SX
Selby	17.06	SX
Welbeck	17.36	SX + SuO
Selby	17.51	SO
Selby	18.38	SX
Selby	19.06	SX + SuO
Selby	19.31	SO
Selby	20.06	SX + SuO
Selby	21.06	SX + SuO
Ellington	21.36	WThFO
Selby	22.06	SX
Selby	22.36	SX + SuO
Selby	22.46	SO
Selby	23.36	SX + SuO

National Power introduced their own Class 59/2 locomotives from April 1994 (as mentioned in Chapter 1) along with an initial fleet of JHA wagons, and later a fleet of similar JMA wagons. Their initial use was to convey limestone from Tunstead for the desulphurisation plant at Drax, but from January 1996, they took over the coal circuits from Gascoigne Wood to Drax and Eggborough, replacing Loadhaul. From 1 July 1997, the Class 59s also started a new 10.19 a.m. Ferrybridge to Maltby Colliery and 1.20 p.m. Maltby to Drax flow. EWS took over National Power's operations, including the

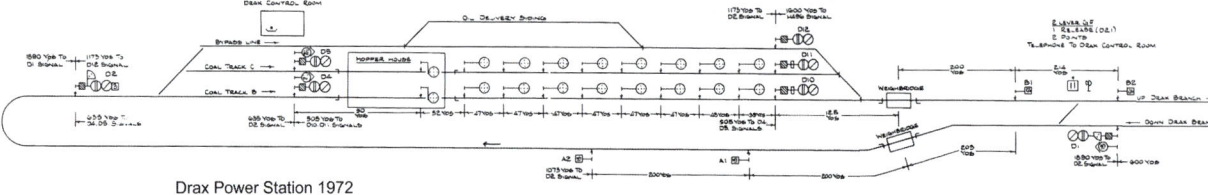

Diagram of signalling layout on the Drax coal circuit.

The only time I visited Drax in the 1990s was on 16 November 1999, and on that date, former National Power 59201 *Vale of York* approaches West Bank crossing on the Drax branch with 6A21 Drax to Gascoigne Wood empties.

Passing the long-closed Carlton Towers station on the Drax branch, 66084 takes another train of coal to the power station, running as 7H53 Kellingley Colliery to Drax on 16 November 1999.

59/2s and JHA/JMA wagons, from April 1998. The locos were repainted in EWS livery and redeployed elsewhere as Class 66s took over their duties. The JHA/JMA wagons were re-bogied, re-coded as HJA and HKA respectively, and also redeployed elsewhere.

Only after the Class 59s started in service did I take an interest in photographing them on the Drax branch. I had previously photographed the National Power services entering and leaving Eggborough power station at Whitley Bridge Junction. On another occasion, I took a few photos at the former Carlton Towers station on the Drax branch itself.

Former National Power 59203 *Vale of Pickering* is seen working a train of empty limestone hoppers that had brought in limestone for the flue gas desulphurisation plant at Drax. The train was 6M96 Drax to Peak Forest, and it is seen as it has just passed the former Carlton Towers station on the Drax branch on 16 November 1999.

The final shot of the day saw 66062 working 6A22 Drax to Milford as it approaches West Bank crossing on the Drax branch on 16 November 1999.

Eggborough

Construction of Eggborough power station started in 1962. The station comprised four 500-MW coal-fired units, giving a total electrical output of 1,960 MW, which started supplying the National Grid in 1967. Eggborough's official opening occurred on 18 September 1970, and the station has gone on to supply around 5 per cent of the country's electricity requirement—equivalent to powering 200 million homes. The Eggborough branch diverged from the Knottingley–Goole line at Whitley Bridge Junction, just east of Whitley Bridge station itself.

Table 10 shows a typical week's coal plan during the latter part of 1993. Although most of the traffic originated from the nearby Selby coalfield, note also the long distance workings from Wearmouth in the north-east. Wearmouth was the last operational pit in the County Durham coalfield, but it closed on 10 December 1993.

Following privatisation, Eggborough was acquired by National Power, but it was bought by British Energy in March 2000. It was due to close in March 2017, but a further contract won it a reprieve until February 2018. However, it failed to win a contract to provide back-up electricity generating capacity for 2018–2019, and Eggborough's fate was therefore sealed. During mid-2021, demolition began and the trackwork was lifted in the power station and transported to the Wensleydale Railway for their use.

Table 10: Typical Week of Eggborough Arrivals, Late 1993		
Origin	Arrive	Days
Selby	00.58	MX
Selby	01.34	MO
Selby	02.16	MX
Harworth	03.23	MX
PoW	09.13	WThFO
Sharlston	11.15	SX
Selby	12.27	SX
Selby	15.57	SX
PoW	16.23	SuO
Wearmouth	18.03	SX
Selby	19.27	SuO
Selby	20.27	WThFO
Wearmouth	21.03	MTO
PoW	22.30	SuO
PoW=Prince of Wales		

National Power 59203 *Vale of Pickering* comes off the Eggborough branch at Whitley Bridge Junction with 6B76 Eggborough to Gascoigne Wood on 18 July 1996.

No. 59202 *Vale of White Horse* passes Whitley Bridge Junction with 6B81 Drax to Gascoigne Wood as 59204 *Vale of Glamorgan* is waiting to leave Eggborough on 18 July 1996.

After 59202 had passed, 59204 *Vale of Glamorgan* comes off the branch at Whitley Bridge Junction with 6B05 Eggborough to Gascoigne Wood on 18 July 1996.

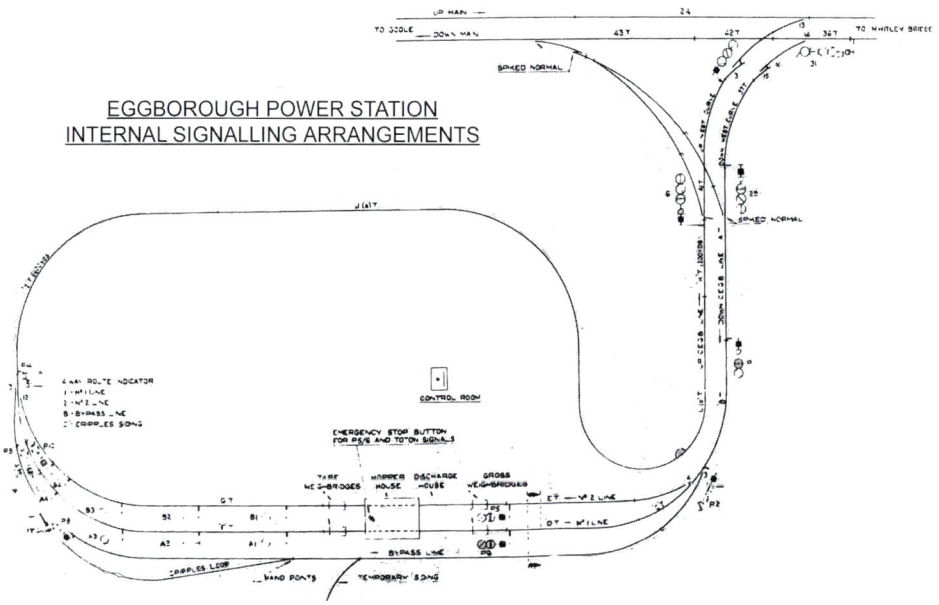

Signalling diagram of the Eggborough power station coal loop.

High Marnham

Consent for construction of High Marnham power station was granted on 22 September 1955 on land occupied by Bark's Farm, between the villages of High Marnham and Fledborough. High Marnham would become the country's first 1,000-MW power station, and the largest coal-fired station under one roof in Europe. Over 2,000 people were employed at the peak of its construction. A new rail spur was installed west of Fledborough station (on the former Lancashire, Derbyshire, and East Coast (LD&EC) line from Shirebrook North to Pyewipe Junction, Lincoln), feeding into a fan of completely new sidings built for the power station. The High Marnham to Fledborough road was re-routed, and a new road-over-rail bridge was constructed a few yards to the south of the existing road bridge.

A new brick signal box, built by British Railways, controlled access to the sidings, and High Marnham was completed in 1962 at a cost of £50 million, although it had started generating back in 1959.

I first visited the power station on 17 June 1993 to photograph 58030 departing with 6H35 High Marnham to Ollerton empties. Between April 1994 and March 1995, the line between Thoresby and High Marnham saw no rail traffic as the power station ran entirely on reclaimed coal for the period.

I was to visit many times between 1995 and 1998, obtaining images of Classes 56, 58, and 60 on coal trains. As I knew some of the Worksop-based drivers, I was fortunate enough to obtain some cab rides through the power station discharge bunker, and a couple more along the entire distance from Ollerton to High Marnham. The power station was mothballed in 2002, and the line between Thoresby Colliery and the power station became unused but trains did eventually begin running again, until the total closure was announced in 2003. Today, the power station has been completely demolished, and the former LD&EC route is now truncated at a point where High Marnham signal box formerly presided.

Table 11: High Marnham Arrivals (Week Commencing 13 September 1998)				
Train	Depart Colliery	Days Run	Colliery Origin	Arrive
7J22	04.36	EWD	Milford#	07.15
7J23	06.26	TX	Milford#	09.15
7J24	08.36	TX	Milford#	11.15
7J25	11.31	MTWO	Thoresby	12.40
7J26	13.36	MSX	Milford#	15.30
# Imported coal ex- Hunterston				

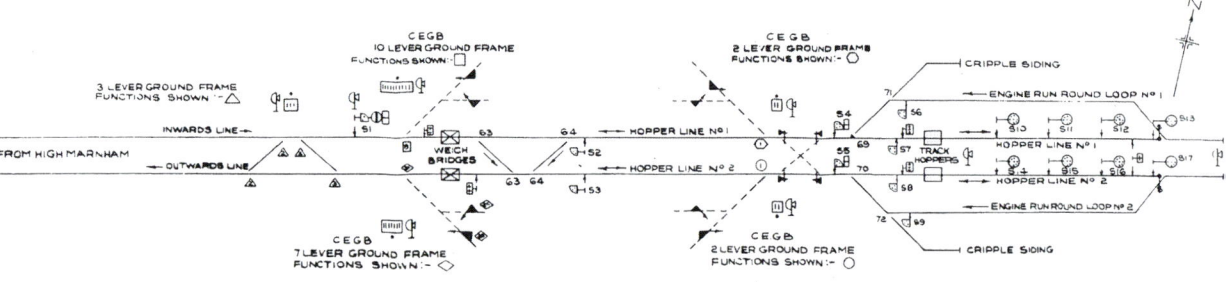

High Marnham power station signalling diagram.

No. 58030 is leaving High Marnham with empties as 6H35 for Ollerton on 17 June 1993. Notice the long redundant loading gauge and ground frames, which were used when the power station sidings were first opened.

As viewed from the Crabtree Lane overbridge and with the power station in the background, 58038 departs High Marnham with 6H35 for Ollerton Colliery on 19 June 1993.

Driven by Worksop driver Bert Ramsdale, 58036 is seen discharging its load of coal at High Marnham power station as 7R63 from Thoresby on 9 June 1995. Bert had seen me stood on the overbridge taking a photo of his train as it approached, so stopped and asked if I wanted a ride—well, you do not need asking twice. So while his train was being discharged, I took photos.

A second view of 58036 at it slowly pulls through the discharge shed on 9 June 1995.

Having dropped me off at the overbridge at High Marnham, I dashed around to Crabtree Lane to get this image of 58036 as it departs from High Marnham with 6W63 for Thoresby; the power station is seen in the background on 9 June 1995.

I returned to the power station a few days later, and instead of using the overbridge as a view point, I walked along the trackbed of the closed section of line towards Lincoln as far as Fledborough Viaduct, where this image was taken. No. 58036 is unloading 7R63 from Thoresby on 22 June 1995, while over to the left, a Terex grading machine works on the coal stocking area.

After discharging its train, 58049 *Littleton Colliery* is seen departing High Marnham with 6K25 empties for Welbeck Colliery on a very cold 20 January 1998.

Ratcliffe-on-Soar

Ratcliffe-on-Soar power station is located adjacent to the Midland Main Line, just south of its crossing over the River Trent. Commissioned in 1968, four Babcock and Wilcox coal-fired boilers each drive a 500-MW Parsons generator set, providing a total generating capacity of 2,116 MW and enough to meet the needs of approximately 2.02 million homes.

The MGR access line leaves the Midland Main Line just south of Red Hill Tunnels. The loop includes a twin-track coal-discharge hopper and an independent line for fly ash operations. Ratcliffe was planned to burn 6.25 million tons of coal *per annum*, supplied by twenty-four trains per day, but by 1981, it was burning 5.5 million tonnes *per annum*, consuming 65 per cent of the output of south Nottinghamshire's collieries.

By 1993, Toton men were working to Ratcliffe, and a typical week's worth of traffic would originate from the collieries shown in Table 12. Table 13 shows the arrivals at the power station for the week beginning 13 September 1998.

Table 12: 1993 Colliery Origin	
Bennerley	13,000 tons
Bentinck	40,000 tons
Calverton	10,500 tons
Rufford	13,500 tons
Thoresby	7,500 tons

Table 13: Ratcliffe Arrivals (Week Commencing 13 September 1998)				
Train ID	Depart Colliery	Days Run	Colliery Origin	Arrive
7A08	05.30	SO	Bentinck	07.30
7A11	08.26	EWD	Calverton	10.28
7A11	09.40	THFO	Doe Hill	10.28
7A11	05.41	SO	Daw Mill	10.52
7A14	10.30	TTHO	Oxcroft	13.30
7A17	13.00	SX	Oxcroft	16.30
7Z61	10.32	SX	Silverdale	19.30
7A23	20.30	MSX	Bentinck	22.30
7A24	19.37	SX	Daw Mill	00.01

Despite its proximity to the M1 motorway and therefore within easy reach, I have only ever visited Ratcliffe twice—both times involving conflict with security. On the first occasion, I parked up on the A453 and walked over a grassed area to the surrounding fence. It was possible to photograph a train curving around the loop following discharge. I had just started photographing such a train when a security van appeared. The security guard emerged from the van, walked across the grass, and confronted me with 'What are you doing?'

Resisting temptation to say something facetious, I replied that I just wanted a photo of the train. Out came the predictable 'It's illegal to take picture from there' retort, but

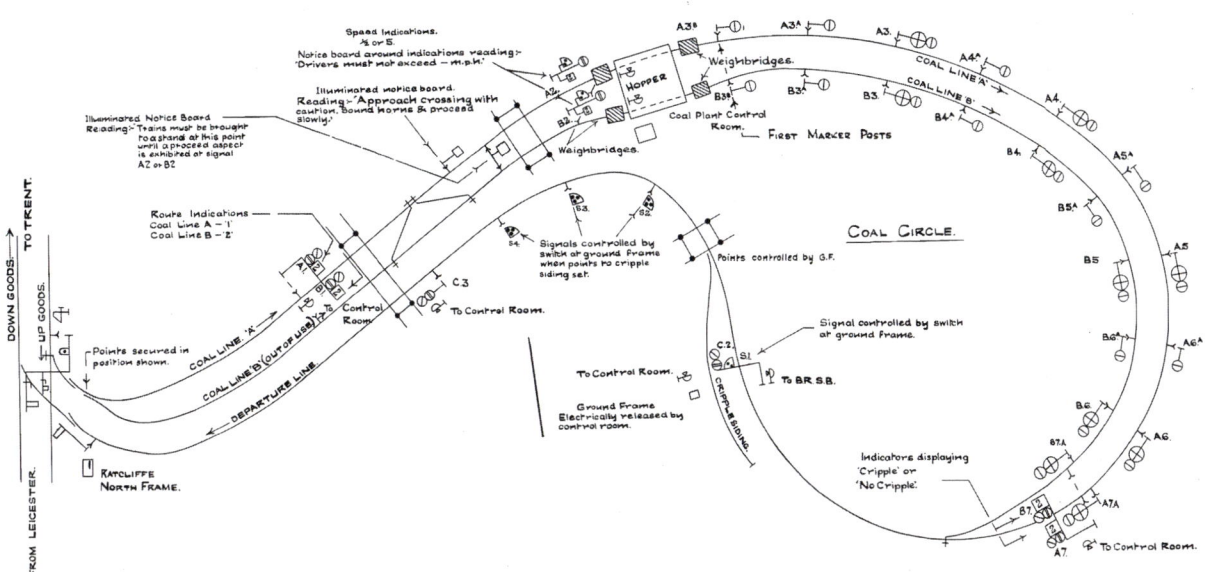

The coal circle signalling at Ratcliffe power station when new.

My first visit to the power station on 11 November 1993 was just in time to see 58022 as it passes through the discharge shed with 7A22 from Thoresby. The single line and shed to the right is the Dust Line, where flyash is loaded to be taken away from the power station.

No. 58022 has now finished discharging, and the driver is putting on power to leave. It was at this point that the security guard made an appearance but was too late as I had taken the photo and was ready to leave myself.

On the second visit to the site, 60076 *Suilven* has just about completed discharging 7A29 from Thoresby and is almost ready to set off back to Toton on 20 June 1994. Notice the large amount of coal stocked on the left.

since I was in a public area, I doubted the credibility of that statement. By that time, the train had moved past and I had my photographs so I just walked away from the security guard, leaving him aghast.

The second occasion was almost a repeat performance, only this time the security guard was much more amiable. After telling him of my intentions, he stood and chatted as I took my photos, and when I left, we almost parted as 'friends'.

Staythorpe

Located next to the River Trent between Southwell and Newark, on the Nottingham to Lincoln line, Staythorpe power station originally consisted of the 112-MW Staythorpe 'A', which was commissioned in July 1950, and the 354 MW Staythorpe 'B', commissioned in May 1962. Coal was received in conventional wagons into sidings on either side of the main line, depending on the direction from which they came. However, access was only possible from the west end at Staythorpe Crossing signal box. Inside the sidings, the BR loco would detach and an internal shunting loco would shunt the loaded wagons into the discharge area, while the BR loco collected an empty set of wagons from the reception sidings. This method of operation continued even after the implementation of MGR operations from May 1982.

In 1972, Staythorpe 'B' apparently held the record for receiving the heaviest train in Britain—6D18 from Newstead Colliery was formed of fifty-five loaded MGR wagons, grossing 2,341 tons with a payload of 1,650 tons.

Staythorpe 'A' was closed on 31 October 1983, and further traffic was purely for the 'B' power station. Subsequent track rationalisation saw the south side sidings removed. Most of the north side sidings were also removed, leaving the arrival/departure roads and five sidings. During the early 1990s, Worksop drivers worked one Staythorpe diagram from Oxcroft. Workings would leave via Seymour Junction to Barrow Hill, then travel south past Chesterfield onto the Erewash Valley line. They diverged at Trowell Junction and headed for Radford Junction towards Nottingham station, from where they travelled to Staythorpe and entered the sidings from the west end. The loco, after running around its train, would propel the wagons back and over the discharge bunker. The coal was carried by conveyor to the power station, which was on the opposite side of the line. The empty train would return to Worksop.

My only visit to Staythorpe was on 15 March 1994 to photograph 58016 arriving with 7J20 from Gascoigne Wood. The final train to enter the sidings was the Branch Line Society's 'Trent Power' rail tour on 26 March 1994, and following Staythorpe 'B' power station's closure later that year, the connections to the arrival/departure lines were taken out of use in October 1994.

```
. STAYTHORPE.    NATPOW.                          W/C 05/12/93
.=====================                            ===========
.
.==============================================================================
. TRIP | TIME | DAYS |   FROM    | REP | TIME | TIME | EMPTIES TO
. NO   | DEP  | RUN  |           ! NO  ! ARR  | DEP  | REMARKS
.------------------------------------------------------------------------------
. TT1S | 0659 | MO   | MANTON    |7J20 | 1007 | 1107 | WORKSOP
.------------------------------------------------------------------------------
. TT1S | 0700 | WFO  | THORESBY  |7J20 | 0855 | 0955 | TOTON
==============================================================================
```

Staythorpe coal plan for week commencing 5 December 1993. (*Courtesy James Skoyles*)

The sidings at Staythorpe were accessed from Staythorpe crossing signal box on the Nottingham to Newark line. Here, 58016 is seen from a public footpath crossing as it is arriving at Staythorpe with 7J20 from Gascoigne Wood on 15 March 1994.

Having uncoupled the loco and run past the train, 58016 is approaching the head shunt adjacent to Staythorpe crossing box on 15 March 1994.

Right: No. 58016 is attached to the other end of its train and will begin to push away from the camera to the discharge area.

Below: No. 58016 pushes back towards the discharge area. There was no signalling at Staythorpe, all the points being hand worked.

Thorpe Marsh

On 16 May 1958, the minister of power gave the go ahead for CEGB's north-eastern region to build Thorpe Marsh power station on a site just north of Doncaster, at a projected cost of £40 million. Work started in 1959, and by 1964, the power station was complete. One of the smaller coal-fired power stations, there were two 550-MW generators powered by a single boiler.

Thorpe Marsh was officially opened on 2 June 1967 by Ernest G Boissier DSC CEng FIEE. Together with Drax, Eggborough, and Ferrybridge 'C', it could produce 25 per cent of the UK's energy requirement during the winter months if required.

The rail access to the power station was originally via the closed Hull & Barnsley and Great Central Joint Railway line to Bullcroft Junction, which was reopened and extended in December 1961. The original rail layout comprised of four exchange sidings for conventional 24.5-ton hoppers, with the wagons being pushed over the discharge pits by the power station's own internal locomotive. This was superseded by a MGR unloading facility in September 1970. The rail link to Bullcroft Junction was closed on 7 September 1970, having been replaced by a new connection from Applehurst Junction. New signalling was installed around the power station sidings, two of which in turn survived until 1994 as emergency storage sidings.

The coal plant could handle two trains at a time, with a maximum unloading capacity of 1,200 tons per hour to the underground bunker, which was then transferred to an 800-ton hopper. The coal store could hold 820,000 tons, which was enough for twelve weeks' supply.

At privatisation, Thorpe Marsh passed into National Power ownership from 16 August 1989. In 1992, 270,000 tons of coal was supplied by Bentley Colliery, 400,000 tons from Hatfield, and supplies also originating from Maltby.

The closure of Thorpe Marsh was announced on 8 June 1993. An eleven-man link of Doncaster Carr Loco-based drivers worked the trains, but following closure, they were left with just Immingham or Drax oil trains. The final train ran on Friday, 11 June 1993, hauled by 56068 from Silverwood Colliery. The final crippled wagons were removed on Saturday, 18 June 1993.

Of the 2.5 million tons of stockpiled coal that remained at the power station, some 200,000 tons were recovered and taken to Eggborough power station. Recovery started from 2 February 1994, shovel loaders being employed to load MGR wagons. The last such train ran on 2 March 1995, hauled by 56087. The site closed on 31 March 1994, and all internal rail signals were decommissioned on 25 November 1994.

The boiler house and other main buildings were demolished in 1996, while the three chimneys were demolished on 14 February 1999. The six cooling towers were demolished on separate occasions during 2012—the south-westernmost on 1 April 2012, the north-easternmost on 10 June 2012, the centre two towers on 5 August 2012, and the last two towers on 19 August 2012.

There had been hope of a renaissance for the sidings during 1999, when ABLE Auto Transport announced an intention to use the site for the transportation of new cars by rail, for onward delivery to local dealers on car transporters. Unfortunately, Doncaster Council put paid to the plan due to inadequate roads in the area, despite a loaded train using the sidings as a test. Access to the former power station site was finally removed in 2007 when the main line points were dispensed with during track relaying.

I never visited Thorpe Marsh power station during its active life, and even after closure I only went three times as access for photography was not easy. To gain a position on the west side of the power station entailed a drive to the village of Thorpe in Balne via narrow roads, along Applehurst Lane and through a farm to the railway. Continuing on foot alongside the railway, a disused railway embankment that formerly crossed the line was climbed, which gave some height to view trains departing from the power station. Another closer view was obtained by passing beneath the line through a cattle creep, then walking alongside the south side of the line to the boundary fence.

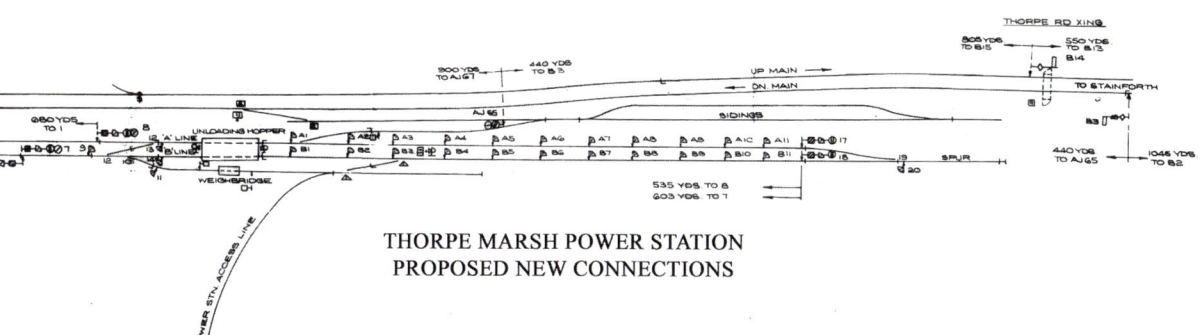

Above: Thorpe Marsh power station signalling diagram.

Right: As viewed from the long-closed Hull and Barnsley Railway overbridge abutments, 56055 is ready to depart Thorpe Marsh power station with 7H20 for Drax on 19 May 1994.

Left: No. 56055 is departing Thorpe Marsh power station with 7H20 for Drax on 19 May 1994.

Below: The next arrival at Thorpe Marsh to be loaded on 19 May 1994 was hauled by 56131 *Ellington Colliery*; it is seen here as it is arriving to load as 7H22 for Drax.

Having found a better location for photos by following a cattle creep beneath the line, I obtained this photo of 56109. It was loading 7H21 the 4.30 p.m. Saturdays excepted departure on 13 June 1994.

No. 56109 is now ready to depart from Thorpe Marsh and head to Drax with 7H21 on 13 June 1994.

West Burton

Located at Sturton, alongside the Sheffield to Lincoln line between Retford and Gainsborough, West Burton was the first 2,000-MW power station to be constructed in the UK. Commissioned between 1967 and 1968, it was officially opened in 1969.

West Burton was the first to operate on the MGR system in 1965. Following discharge from the HAA wagons into below-track hoppers, remotely-operated paddle feeder machines scooped the coal evenly along the length of the hoppers onto two twin belt conveyors. They fed the coal to the screening and crushing plant (where it is also passed through magnetic separators) where further conveyors took it to the transfer tower. Here the coal was either fed directly to the boiler house or onto the stockpile for later use. The stockpile had a maximum capacity of 2 million tons, standing some 30 feet deep, which was enough for over three months' operation.

West Burton signal box was opened by British Rail in 1964 to control both access and egress to the power station and around the internal loop. West Burton was unusual in that there was access from both the east and the west, which allowed a degree of flexibility if one or the other routes was unavailable—diverted trains would pass the power station and run around at either Gainsborough Central or Worksop, depending on the direction from which they originated.

Initially, coal was received from the Shirebrook, Worksop, and Barrow Hill areas, but later on, supplies originated both from Scotland and from imports. Table 14 shows a typical weekly coal programme for West Burton for week commencing Sunday, 15 April 1990, while Table 15 is dated September 1994.

Table 14: West Burton Power Station Train List (Week Commencing 15 April 1990)					
Train	Depart Colliery	Days Run	Colliery Origin	Power Station Arrive/Depart	Train Recess/Next Working
7G50	05.26	ThFO	Thoresby	07.45　08.55	Warsop Jn
7G52	06.28	WThFO	Welbeck	08.30　09.40	Warsop Jn
7G54	06.40	ThFO	Harworth	09.15　10.25	Worksop
7G56	07.50	TWThO	Shireoaks	10.00　11.10	Worksop
7G58	08.36	WThFO	Thoresby	10.45　11.55	Warsop Jn
7G60	09.29	TO	Welbeck	11.41　12.51	Shirebrook Sdgs
7G60	09.28	WThFO	Welbeck	11.30　12.40	Shirebrook Sdgs
7G64	10.54	MSX	Maltby	13.00　14.10	Worksop
7G66	11.26	WThFO	Thoresby	13.45　14.55	Warsop Jn
7G68	12.56	MSX	Kiveton	14.30　15.40	Worksop
7G74	14.43	MSX	Welbeck	16.45　17.55	Warsop Jn
7G76	15.24	MSX	Maltby	17.30　18.40	Worksop
7G78	15.40	WFO	Harworth	18.15　19.45	Worksop
7G80	17.26	ThO	Kiveton	19.00　20.10	Worksop
7G82	17.36	WThSO	Thoresby	19.45　20.55	Thoresby
7G84	18.24	MSX	Maltby	20.30　21.40	Worksop
7G88	19.58	MSX	Welbeck	22.00　23.10	Shirebrook Sdgs

7G92	21.24	TThO	Maltby	23.30	00.40	Worksop
7G32	22.58	TWThO	Welbeck	01.00	02.10	Welbeck
7G32	22.58	FO	Welbeck	01.00	02.10	Warsop Jn
7G34	23.36	WThO	Thoresby	01.45	03.55	Thoresby
7G34	23.36	FO	Thoresby	01.45	03.55	Warsop Jn

Table 15: West Burton Typical Week in September 1994			
Code	Origin	Arrive	Days
7G30	Harworth	00.30	TWThO
7G31	Thoresby	01.30	TWThO
7G32	Bilsthorpe	02.30	MO
7G32	Worksop 1	02.30	TThO
7G32	Worksop 2	02.30	WO
7G33	Harworth	04.30	FSX
7G34	Thoresby	07.30	MTWO
7G34	Bilsthorpe	08.30	ThO
7G34	Harworth	10.30	SO
7G35	Kiveton	10.30	SX
7G35	Bilsthorpe	11.30	SO
7G36	Thoresby	11.30	MTWO
7G37	Clipstone	12.30	MTWSO
7G37	Kiveton	12.30	THFO
7G38	Worksop 3	15.30	MTWO
7G38	Bilsthorpe	15.30	SO
7G39	Bilsthorpe	16.30	MTWO
7G39	Harworth	16.30	SO
7G40	Thoresby	17.30	MWO
7G40	Clipstone	17.30	SO
7G41	Bilsthorpe	18.30	SO
7G41	Clipstone	18.30	MTWO
7G42	Kiveton	18.30	MTWO
7G41	Thoresby	19.30	SuO
7G42	Bilsthorpe	23.30	SuO
7G43	Worksop 4	23.30	MTO
7G43	Clipstone	23.30	WO
1 = ex-Silverwood, 2 = ex-Clipstone, 3 = ex-Welbeck, 4 = ex-Bilsthorpe			

My experiences with West Burton started in 1981, when I took up a signalling position at Worksop West signal box. One of the requirements of the job was to know your area, so I made it my duty to obtain a cab ride from Worksop to West Burton to see the railway from the driver's perspective. At the time, trains were departing from Worksop for the power stations fairly regularly, so all I needed to do was to walk to the yard outlet signal and climb aboard a loco—back in BR days, there was no requirement for a cab ride pass or any form of identification.

After arrival at West Burton, I found there was time to climb down as the train was one of four awaiting discharge. As the process took sixty minutes, I walked to the unloading bunker to see the train ahead being emptied. I should note that at no point during my wander around West Burton was I ever challenged—something unheard of today. Not only was I able to watch the discharge process, but I could also go to the hopper below track level to watch the paddles scoop the coal onto the conveyors. From there, I made my way across to the boiler room to watch how the boilers were fed. Alas, I was without a camera that day so the whole process went totally unrecorded.

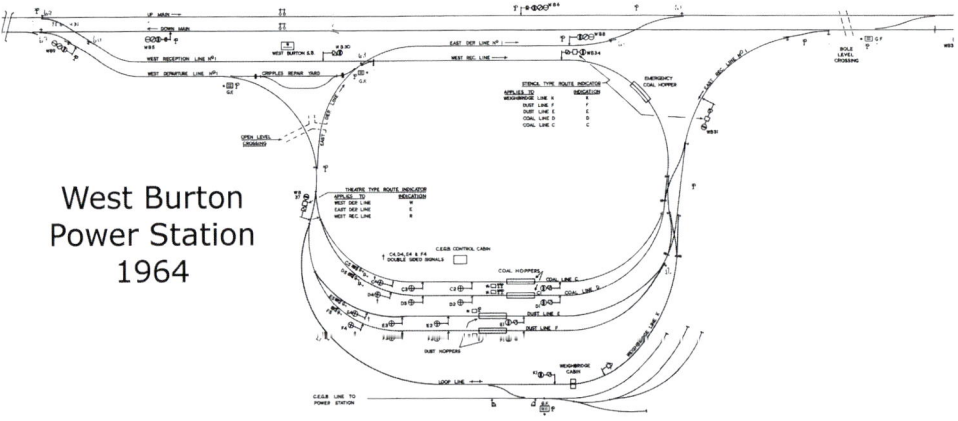

Above: West Burton power station signalling diagram.

Below: After bringing in and discharging 7G50 Clipstone Colliery to West Burton on Saturday, 28 October 1995, 58031 was stabled in the power station for the weekend and is seen here on Sunday, 29 October 1995. The building to the right is the two-track ash disposal point.

As viewed from West Burton signal box, 58025 arrives at the power station with another load of Nottinghamshire's finest coal from Clipstone Colliery on a sunny day in August 1996.

Another view from the signal box sees 'Dutch'-liveried 56036 departing for Worksop on 11 February 1994.

A view from the cab as a train enters the discharge bunker at West Burton. This image is later than the 1990s, but apart from the orange-clad workers, the view has not changed.

Not really a coal train but worth a look anyway. In connection with Worksop open day on 5 September 1993, a series of shuttle trains were run, and here as viewed from the train, 37504 and 37202 are seen as they are running through West Burton power station.

After discharging its train, 58010 leaves the west end of West Burton with 6G36 empties for Worksop on 5 May 1993. The building to the left is the former crossing keeper's house dating from when there was a level crossing across the line here.

No. 58036 snakes away from the west departure line with 6G35 for Worksop on 2 June 1994.

Above: Shortly after departing West Burton power station, the driver of 58009 puts on power as he takes 6W67 back to Worksop on 2 April 1996.

Below: A snapshot in time from the train register book at West Burton signal box for a twelve-hour period on one day in 1998. The signalman going off duty was Julian Marshall, being relieved by Paul Cooke. Paul has annotated the remarks column with the loco numbers beside the train headcodes, which nicely gives an indication of the types of locos being used at the time.

Willington

Willington power station was built in the 1950s close to the junction of the Derby–Burton line and that from Trent Junction at Stenson Junction. The complex actually comprised of two almost entirely independent coal-fired generating stations on the same site. Both were managed and staffed separately, with only coal and water supplies being shared between the two. Willington 'A', which was closest to the main road, came on line in 1957 and used two of the five cooling towers. Its counterpart, Willington 'B', came on line a few years later and used the remaining three cooling towers.

On 11 August 1981, 47329 hauling thirty-five loaded HAA wagons from Denby Opencast site marked the inauguration of MGR operations, with a special ceremony held to mark the opening of the £9-million unloading facility. In 1989, Willington was privatised and sold to National Power.

Willington was mothballed several times. It received coal from Denby, Bilsthorpe, and Markham during June and July 1992, but at the time, the power station was only working during daylight hours, generating at around half of its design capacity.

As mentioned in Chapter 1, there was a metaphorical 'Berlin Wall' demarcation line that existed at Shirebrook between London Midland and Eastern Region depots. One train that crossed this invisible boundary was 7B78 on the 5.18 p.m. (Friday and Saturday excepted) Bilsthorpe Colliery to Willington. This was worked by a Worksop driver (from the Eastern Region) from Bilsthorpe Colliery as far as Shirebrook, from where a Toton driver (from the London Midland Region) would take the train forwards to Willington for arrival at 7.26 p.m. Following discharge, the driver would take the train at 9.45 p.m. back to Toton. The following day the train would be taken to Shirebrook by a Toton driver, from where a Worksop driver would take it forward to Bilsthorpe for reloading, after which the same Worksop driver would take the train as far as Shirebrook for the cycle to repeat again.

In July 1992, BR were reported to have asked National Power for money in order to re-model the power station access lines, but National Power refused to pay out. Consequently, the departure lines were physically blocked and coal traffic ceased on 17 July 1992. The final delivery was hauled by 56021 from Denby, and that afternoon, 58015 arrived to remove some 'green carded' wagons for repair. That was not quite the end, as services resumed for a short while due to contractual reasons.

What was reported to be the final train ran on 19 April 1993 as 7D48 07.30 Markham to Willington, hauled by 60088. The empties later worked to Derby for a crew change. 56004 arrived later in the day to remove the final crippled wagons to Burton-on-Trent wagon repair depot. While this should have been the end, it was not as I photographed a train in the power station in 1994.

The connections into the power station from Stenson Junction were severed on 11 September 1994. Bizarrely, the weekly coal plan still showed two trains for Willington in 1998, although these were shown as 'suspended'. While giving an idea of the booked traffic during the power station's latter days, Table 16 shows the projected planned arrivals for week commencing 13 September 1998.

```
         *********
L.M. COAL ALLOCATIONS TO SPECIFIC USERS    W/C : 31/10/93
=============================================================
WILLINGTON. NATPOW
==================
=============================================================
TRIP! DEP  ! DAYS !   FROM      !REP NO! TIME  ! TIME  ! EMPTIES
 NO ! TIME ! RUN  !              !      ! ARR   ! DEP   ! TO
-------------------------------------------------------------
 T2W! 0830 ! MWFO ! LOUNGE       ! 6D55 ! 1032  ! 1206  ! TOTON
-------------------------------------------------------------
 T1W! 1038 ! SX   ! MILFORD      ! 6D57 ! 1300  ! 1434  ! TOTON
=============================================================
```

Willington coal plan for week commencing 31 October 1993. (*Courtesy James Skoyles*)

Table 16: Willington Arrivals (Week Commencing 13 September 1998)					
Service Suspended					
Code	Time	Days	Origin	Destination	Arrive
6T49	10.40	SX	Toton	Milford	12.40
7D49	15.20	SX	Milford #	Willington	08.00
6P49	10.00	MX	Willington	Toton	11.00
6K42	11.55	SX	Worksop	Hull	14.35
7D52	16.50	SX	Hull	Worksop	21.01
7D52	09.00	MX	Worksop	Willington	11.00
6P52	13.00	MX	Willington	Worksop	15.00
#Traffic ex-Wardley loaded by Knottingley Crews					

Station 'A' was de-synchronised from the National Grid on 30 September 1994, with formal closure following on 31 May 1995. Willington 'B' was to be de-synchronised on 31 March 1999, and although the main part of the power station was demolished, the cooling towers remain to this day.

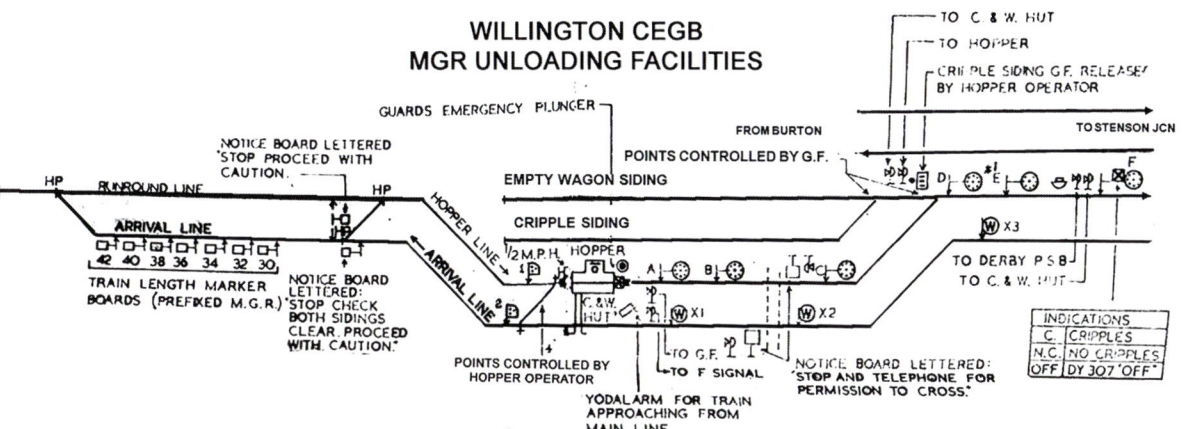

Section of diagram issued to drivers regarding the new Willington CEGB MGR unloading facilities. (*Ian Farnfield Collection*)

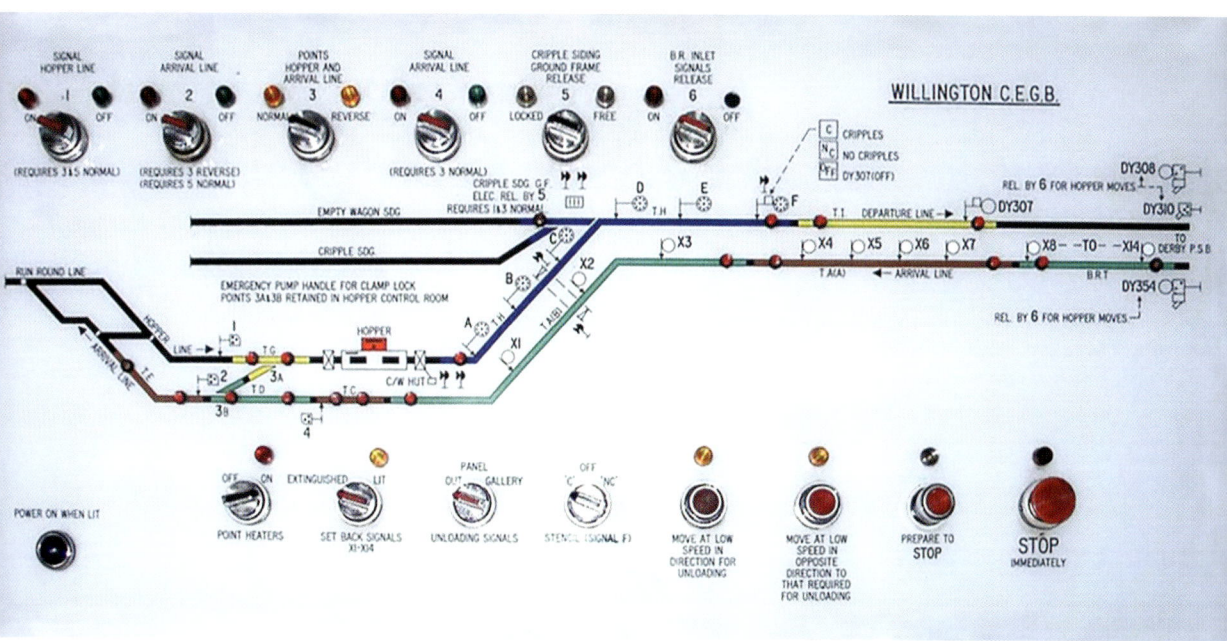

A photograph of the signalling panel at Willington power station. (*Courtesy of Nick Allsop*)

The only time I managed a photo of a train in Willington power station was this one on 11 July 1994. Having finished discharging 7H97 Milford to Willington, the train preparer walks back along the train as the driver of 58048 *Coventry Colliery* waits to take the empty train to Toton.

Above: A very backlit view of 58048 *Coventry Colliery* as it departs from Willington for Toton on 11 July 1994.

Below: The driver puts on power and heads towards the exit from the power station on 11 July 1994. The cooling towers on the left almost look to be covered in camouflage paint but is in fact a result of weathering.

8

Three Days at Worksop

To finish off this book, I thought it might be good to look back at a moment in time at Worksop, to see how busy the area still was even at the end of the twentieth century.

The movement of coal had been the lifeblood of Worksop depot for many years, and as the 1990s ended, it was still the *raison d'être*. Who then would have thought that the coal industry would totally collapse a mere fifteen years later, and that Worksop depot would close in October 2015?

In 2017, while having a clear-out at Worksop power signal box where I worked, I came across part of a faded fax document sent out on Wednesday, 3 March 1999. A look at the destination of empties from Worksop Yard that it showed will round the decade off nicely.

The document had faded badly, being one of those faxes on heated paper, but with a few exceptions almost three days' worth of traffic could still be made out. As such, I extrapolated what information was legible to see where these Worksop drivers went to. Table 17 is a representation of the document.

Although Worksop had been re-signalled in 1997, most of the photos in this selection show the semaphore signals that still existed beforehand. The yard was part of the EWS Empire at the time, and trains were primarily hauled by Class 58s, and Class 56s to a greater or lesser extent, although Class 66s were beginning to make an inroad.

Table 17: List Sent Out on Wednesday, 3 March 1999		
Wednesday		
Train	Depart	Destination
6K68	12.18	Harworth
6K29	12.45	Milford
6K69	12.48	Clipstone

6K72	15.17	Milford
0Y42	17.30	Bolsover Coalite
6K74	18.00	Harworth
6P00	1824	Toton
6K52	18.36	Rossington
6K77	20.17	Doncaster Decoy
Thursday		
6Y40	00.37	Gas Wood
6K58	00.57	Milford
6K59	01.17	Rossington
6K03	02.07	Milford
(Information missing)		
6T69	12.17	Milford
6K68	12.18	Harworth
6K74	12.31	Immingham C.P.
6K93	12.38	Oxcroft
6K29	12.45	Milford
6K70	12.51	Rossington
6K95	15.04	Oxcroft
6K72	15.17	Milford
(Information missing)		
0Y42	17.30	Bolsover Coalite
6P00	18.24	Washwood Heath
6K52	18.36	Rossington
6K77	20.17	Milford
Friday		
6K92	08.33	Doe Hill
6K91	08.50	Hatfield
6G77	09.20	Harworth
6K66	09.27	Maltby
6K26	10.58	Rossington
6K94	12.00	Hatfield
6K68	12.18	Harworth
6K29	12.45	Milford
6K69	12.48	Clipstone
6K70	12.51	Rossington
6K72	15.17	Milford
0Y42	17.30	Bolsover Coalite
6K74	18.00	Harworth
6P00	18.24	Toton Up Side
6K52	18.36	Rossington

Harworth-Bound

The first train on the list that could be properly discerned was due out from Worksop Down Yard at 12.18 p.m. as 6K68 for Harworth Colliery. Assuming that the train was hauled by a Class 58, it would leave Worksop Down Yard and join Down Departure No. 1, to stand at WP621 signal at Shireoaks East Junction to await the passage of the Down Lincoln to Sheffield passenger train that departed Worksop at 12.15 p.m. Once the passenger had passed WP531 signal, WP621 signal would clear to a single yellow aspect and the 'Theatre' indicator would show 'M', indicating to the driver that the route was set for the 'Main' line; if 'B' was shown on the indicator, the route was set for the 'Branch' to Shirebrook.

The driver now applying power and releasing the brakes, the train would slowly depart from Worksop and proceed towards Shireoaks. After the station, the driver would slow for the 15-mph speed restriction over Brancliffe East Junction. The signal on the approach, WP523, was 'approach-controlled' (only releasing to a 'proceed' green aspect when the track circuit approaching it was occupied by the train); when the 'proceed' aspect was lit with its associated route indicator (colloquially known as a 'feather'), the train was routed from the Down Main to the Down South Yorkshire Joint Railway. Power would now be applied for the 1-in-100 climb to Dinnington Junction. Between Brancliffe East Junction and Dinnington Junction, the route was double track, but was single track from there to Maltby.

Owing to the density of traffic then using the South York's line, the driver might have to wait at WP607 signal at Dinnington Junction for a train coming from Maltby to clear the single line section before he would get the signal to proceed.

Above left: Before re-signalling, 58012 departs from Worksop down side for Harworth as viewed from Shireoaks East signal box on 2 December 1997.

Above right: With the new WP621 waiting commissioning in front of Shireoaks East Junction's semaphore signals, 58022 departs from the down departure No. 2 line at Shireoaks East with a train for Milford on 2 December 1997.

Above left: Before re-signalling, 58015 is seen while standing at Dinnington Colliery Junction signals with 6G54 for Maltby Colliery on 29 December 1995.

Above right: No. 58036 is approaching the site of Anston Junction on the South Yorkshire Joint Railway with 6F88 Worksop to Silverwood Colliery on 7 February 1994.

Below left: No. 56054 *British Steel Llanwern* with 6W02 Worksop to Maltby Colliery crosses Brookhouse Viaduct on 9 October 1997.

Below right: No. 58048 *Coventry Colliery* with 6G38 Worksop to Harworth Colliery approaches Firbeck Junction on 25 April 1995.

Continuing towards Maltby, the train would pass through the remains of Dinnington station before crossing the high steel lattice Brookhouse Viaduct. After Slade Hooton, the remaining platforms of the 1929-closed Maltby Station are passed. On the left was Maltby Colliery, with the rapid loader bunker line converging from the left. Passing Maltby Colliery South signal box on the right, the line swings eastwards and approaches Firbeck Junction, where the train would take the Harworth Branch towards the colliery. The branch is also single, but the junction was formerly triangular which allowed trains from the Doncaster direction to gain the branch directly. With the removal of the northern arm of the triangle, trains for the Doncaster direction had to travel from Harworth to Maltby to run round before heading north again.

One for Milford

Meanwhile, the yard staff would have been preparing to despatch 6K29, the 12.45 p.m. departure to Milford. Taking the same route as the previous train, it would instead take the main line at Firbeck Junction towards St Catherine's Junction. Heading through Doncaster Decoy Yard and thence Doncaster station, the train would take the ECML north as far as Shaftholme Junction, before diverging left and taking the Askern Branch towards Knottingley.

At Knottingley South Junction, the train would bear left, passing Knottingley Depot and Knottingley Station, and diverge right at Knottingley West Junction to head towards Ferrybridge North Junction. Passing Ferrybridge power station and through Brotherton Tunnel, the line from Castleford converged from the left at Burton Salmon. The train's destination within sight, at Milford Junction, the train would be routed off the main line into Milford West Sidings, where it would terminate.

At Milford, the loco would be detached and coupled to a loaded Anglo-Scottish coal train that had arrived from Scotland for recessing at Milford. The train would retrace its steps back in the Worksop direction, destined either for Cottam or West Burton power station.

No. 56131 *Ellington Colliery* passes the then-new Royal Mail terminal at Doncaster Down Decoy with 7C03 Harworth to Eggborough power station on 5 November 1996

Above left: No. 58033 is seen passing through Doncaster station with a loaded MGR service destined for Worksop and then West Burton power station on 7 March 1993.

Above right: No. 58030 passes Doncaster Belmont and takes the line through Doncaster Down Decoy with 7F87 Gascoigne Wood to Cottam power station on 5 November 1996.

Clipstone Calls

Three minutes after the Milford departure was 6K69 at 12.48 p.m. for Clipstone Colliery. Emerging from the Down yard again, the train would receive a green aspect at WP621 signal but now with a 'B' for 'Branch' in the theatre indicator, as the route was set for Woodend Junction and towards Shirebrook. Taking the left-hand curve, the single line from Shireoaks West Junction converged from the right at Woodend Junction. The train is now travelling south on the Up Mansfield line.

Power would now be applied, and the site of Steetley Colliery (closed 1990) is passed on the right. The first of the stations reopened for Robin Hood line services in May 1998 is passed at Whitwell. On the left, just before the train plunges into Whitwell Tunnel, was the site of Whitwell Colliery which succumbed in 1986.

At the other end of the tunnel is Creswell. The train passes Elmton and Creswell signal box, followed by Creswell station—another Robin Hood line reopening. After passing beneath a road overbridge, Creswell Colliery was formerly on the right. A 1991 closure, its rapid-loading bunker was actually on the left of the line.

Following the crossing keeper-controlled Norwood Crossing is another Robin Hood line station at Langwith Whaley-Thorns. The driver would soon start slowing for Shirebrook East Junction to take the single line curve towards Warsop Junction, on the line to Clipstone. The disused Warsop Yard is passed on the left, followed by the double-track curve from Shirebrook Junction converging from the right at Warsop Junction.

No. 58001 takes 6F45 to Clipstone round the curve at Woodend Junction and is passing the site of Woodend Junction box on 19 February 1994.

No. 58022 is passing the site of Steetley Colliery with 6C15 Worksop to Thoresby on 23 March 1995.

Above left: On 28 April 1994, 58023 with 6G15 Worksop to Thoresby is passing the remains of the closed Elmton and Creswell station, which would reopen on the same site in 1998.

Above right: No. 58012 passes Whitwell with 6K70 Worksop to Welbeck as viewed from the top of Whitwell tunnel on 2 May 1997.

The line now crosses a large embankment at Warsop Vale. Prior to crossing the A60 road, the line passes the site of Warsop Colliery on the left. After the road bridge was the long-closed but mostly intact Warsop station.

At Welbeck Colliery Junction, the branch converging from the left unsurprisingly comes from Welbeck Colliery, then still a very active colliery. The train would soon start slowing for Clipstone West Junction and the tight, check-railed, right-hand curve. The western curve passes Clipstone West Junction signal box and joins the former Mansfield Railway at Clipstone South Junction. Now heading towards Rufford Junction, the line passes the site of Mansfield Concentration sidings, which closed in the 1980s. At Rufford Junction, the train will be signalled to take the Clipstone run-round loop.

Coming to a stand here, the driver would propel his train back along the Clipstone Colliery branch to the loading pad. The train would now be loaded with the aid of mechanical shovels. Further images of Clipstone Colliery can be found in Chapter 3.

The loaded train would return to the loop for the loco to run around. It would then return the same way towards Worksop and either recess in the Up yard or continue direct to a power station.

You can read more about the Mansfield Railway and the colliery connections in the author's book, *The Lancashire Derbyshire and East Coast Railway: A LD&ECR Miscellany, the Mansfield Railway and Mid-Nott's Joint Railway Connections* from Fonthill Media.

No. 58015 with 6Y15 Worksop to Welbeck Colliery is rounding the 1974-built connection from the Worksop–Shirebrook Line to the former LD&ECR line at Shirebrook West Junction on 12 May 1994.

No. 58031 is passing Welbeck Colliery Junction with 7G62 Bentinck Colliery to Rufford Stock Site on 6 May 1994, prior to re-signalling of the area in 1997. Another train is waiting to back off the Welbeck Colliery branch in the background.

Above left: No. 58035 rounds the western curve and passes Clipstone West Junction box with 6C44 for Rufford Colliery on 2 May 1994.

Above right: No. 58019 *Shirebrook Colliery* is passing the site of Mansfield Concentration Sidings with 6Y44 for Clipstone Colliery on 29 June 1995.

Next Trains

The next departure was 6K72 at 3.17 p.m. for Milford, which would take the same routing as the earlier departure, followed by a lull in proceedings. The peace was shattered by the despatch of 0Y42 for Bolsover Coalite. While the actions of this loco were described in Chapter 4, its route from the yard was west on the main line via Kiveton to Woodhouse to reverse in the sidings there. It would then take the Beighton line and the Old Road as far as Foxlow Junction, taking the left-hand curve to Hall Lane Junction. It would continue to Seymour Junction and along the Bolsover branch to the Coalite plant.

6P00 Cripple Tripper

A further Harworth-bound train departed as 6K74 at 6 p.m., and at 6.24 p.m., the yard would despatch 6P00. This was destined either for Toton Yard or Washwood Heath in order to take repaired wagons out and to collect crippled wagons for repair at Worksop wagon repair depot. Departing the yard towards Woodend Junction, 6P00 would take the Up Mansfield past Shirebrook, Mansfield, and Kirkby as far as Kirkby Lane End Junction. While the Robin Hood line diverges left, 6P00 bears right and heads towards the Erewash Valley line, passing the Bentinck Colliery branch

Above left: No. 58009 passes Creswell with 6P00 Worksop to Toton empties on 4 June 1997.

Above right: No. 58003 is seen at Stenson junction with a loaded train for Ironbridge power station on 11 July 1994. The tracks on the right side are the access to Willington power station.

(controlled by Pinxton signal box) and Sleights East signal box. Joining the Erewash Valley line at Pye Bridge Junction, 6P00 would head south past Langley Mill and Ilkeston, passing Trowell Junction where the Nottingham line diverges left, to Toton Up yard where it would terminate.

Later in the week, 6P00 would run to Washwood Heath. The above route would be taken again as far as Toton, but the train would now continue beyond to Trent Junction. Negotiating the complex triangle, 6P00 would be routed onto the Castle Donnington line at Sheet Stores Junction, passing the site of Castle Donnington power station on the left. Joining the Derby to Birmingham line at Stenson Junction, the closed Willington power station is passed on the left.

6P00 continues past North Staffordshire Junction (where the Crewe line diverges right) and onwards through Burton-on-Trent, Tamworth High Level, and Water Orton to arrive at its destination—Washwood Heath Up sidings. Here, repaired wagons would be detached and any crippled wagons collected, before beginning the long return journey to Worksop.

Rossington

The next departure from the yard, 6K52 to Rossington Colliery, was at 6.36 p.m. Departing west on the main line towards Shireoaks, its route was identical to that of the Milford workings as far as Doncaster Down Decoy, where it would run around.

It would then head south-east along the ECML along the bi-directional Up West Slow/Down Slow, then past D196 signal. This showed a permanent red aspect, but a position light signal would control access to the run-round loop at Rossington Colliery Junction. The loco would now propel the train along the colliery branch to the loading pad, where loading would take place by mechanical shovel.

The method of propelling along the branch continued after privatisation until a mishap called for a change in operating procedure. Contractors working for RJB Mining started to change some rails without informing the train operators. Unfortunately, an empty MGR train was being propelled along the branch at that exact moment, resulting in the inevitable derailment. Subsequently, the method of working was changed, such that trains either had to be top-and-tailed with locos, or have a brake van attached for the propelling movement. Further photos of Rossington will have been seen in Chapter 5.

After loading, the train would return to the run-round loop for the loco to run around its train. Procedure complete, the driver would use the signal post telephone (SPT) at D193 signal to inform the signaller they were ready to proceed. Departing north-west along the Up West Slow/Down Slow, the loco would run round its train again at Down Decoy and retrace its route along the South York's Line to Worksop and to one of the power stations.

Some trains would take a different route from Down Decoy. Travelling beneath the South York's line, they would take the Down Lincoln flyover over the ECML towards Bessacarr Junction, and onwards via Finningley and Beckingham to Gainsborough. Joining the former MS&L route from Retford at Gainsborough Trent Junction, the train would continue over MS&L metals to Gainsborough Central to perform yet another run round manoeuvre. The final leg of the journey would see the train enter West Burton power station from the eastern entrance. One such working can be seen in Table 18.

Table 18: Rossington to West Burton via Gainsborough					
Code	Depart	Days	Origin	Destination	Arrive
6K63	05.17	SX	Worksop	Rossington	07.27
7B63	08.38	SX	Rossington	West Burton	12.20
Run round Doncaster Down Decoy 09.16–10.35					
Run round Gainsborough Central 11.14–11.34					
6W63	13.30	EWD	West Burton	Worksop	14.01

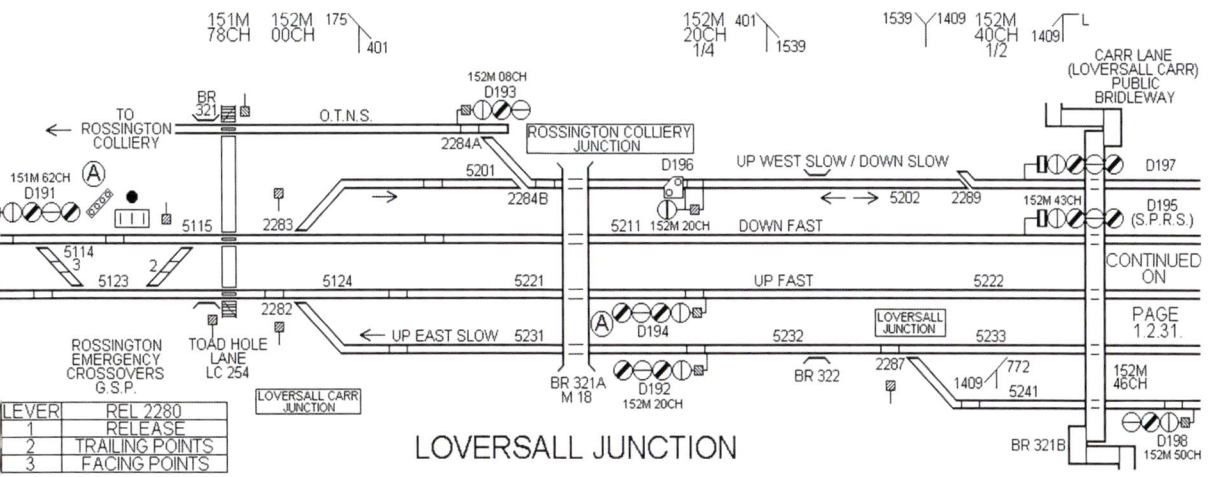

Section of Doncaster PSB panel showing the connections to Rossington Colliery as mentioned in the text.

No. 58045 detaches from its set of wagons to run around 6K66 Worksop to Rossington Colliery at Doncaster Down Decoy on 5 November 1996.

No. 58027 working 7B66 Gascoigne Wood to West Burton runs around its train at Gainsborough Central on 29 January 1998.

After the run around was complete, 58027 now takes 7B66 Gascoigne Wood to West Burton away from Gainsborough Central on 29 January 1998.

Into the Evening, and Ready for the Night Shift

The final evening departure would now be prepared for despatch. 6K77 would depart at 8.17 p.m. to Doncaster Decoy, consisting of empty HAA wagons. The same route to Doncaster Decoy Yard would be taken, where the wagons would be left and the loco would return light engine to Worksop. This working was often due to a lack of spare wagons on the Aire Valley circuits at Sudforth Lane, and the wagons would be collected by a loco sent from Knottingley depot. The train would then load at either Maltby or Rossington collieries, and afterwards head north to one of the Aire Valley power stations.

The night shift now takes duty in Worksop Yard and the cycle of trains continues. At 12.37 a.m., 6Y40 calls out with empties for Gascoigne Wood. The route is identical to the earlier departures for Milford Yard, except 6Y40 passes the yard and continues to the Gascoigne Wood loading area, making a subsequent fully-laden consist for Bolsover Coalite. Twenty minutes later, 6K58 departs at 12.57 a.m. for Milford. Subsequent trains leave at 1.17 a.m. for Rossington and at 2.07 a.m. for Milford again, and the ceaseless procession of departures would continue into Thursday morning and afternoon. Table 17 shows the other trains that ran on the three days in question.

Conclusion

It is lamentable to think that this traffic no longer exists. The coal industry, British Rail and (later) the private freight-operating companies played their part in modernising the movement of black diamonds from pit to power station through the introduction of rapid-loading, automated unloading and high-capacity bogie hopper wagons. Sadly, external politics, and the quest for cleaner and more renewable methods of electricity generation, have sounded the death knell for most of the collieries and coal fired power stations. Kellingley Colliery, the final deep-pit coal mine in Britain, closed on 18 December 2015, bringing to an end the deep mining of coal in this country.

I hope that the reader will take a journey through time and rekindle memories of the sights of coal traffic seen throughout the country that are, regrettably, consigned to history. Importantly, I hope that the reader has enjoyed reading this book as much as I have enjoyed writing it.

Bibliography

Amos, D. and Braber, N., *Bradwell's Images of Coal Mining in the East Midlands* (Bradwell Books, 2017)

Booth, C., *The Lancashire Derbyshire and East Coast Railway: A LD&ECR Miscellany, the Mansfield Railway and Mid-Nott's Joint Railway Connections* (Fonthill Media, 2020)

Booth, C., *The Lancashire Derbyshire and East Coast Railway: Chesterfield to Langwith Junction, the Beighton Branch and Sheffield District Railway* (Fonthill Media, 2017)

Booth, C., *The Lancashire Derbyshire and East Coast Railway: Langwith Junction to Lincoln and the Route to Sutton-on-Sea* (Fonthill Media, 2018)

Downes, E., *Yorkshire Collieries 1947–1994* (Think Pit Publications, 2016)

Monk-Steel, D., *Merry-Go-Round, on the rails* (Historical Model Railway Society, 2011)

Rawlinson, M., *Freightmaster Summer/Autumn 1997* (Freightmaster Publishing, 1997)

Shannon, P., *Railfreight since 1968-Coal* (Silverlink Publishing, 2006)